The Freddie Mercury Story
Living on the Edge

Other titles by David Bret
published by Robson books

The Piaf Legend
The Mistinguett Legend
Maurice Chevalier
Marlene, My Friend
Morrissey: Landscapes of the Mind
Gracie Fields: The Authorized Biography
Tallulah Bankhead: A Scandalous Life

The
Freddie Mercury
Story

Living on the Edge

David Bret

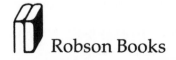

Robson Books

First published in Great Britain in 1996 by Robson
Books Ltd, Bolsover House, 5–6 Clipstone Street,
London W1P 8LE

British Library Cataloguing in Publication Data
A catalogue record for this title is available from the
British Library

ISBN 1 86105 054 2

Photoset in North Wales by Derek Doyle & Associates,
Mold, Flintshire.
Printed and bound in Great Britain by Butler & Tanner,
Frome and London

This book is dedicated to
David Evans, Louise Dixon
and Les Enfants de Novembre

N'oubliez pas . . .
La vie sans amis
c'est comme un
jardin sans fleurs

Contents

Acknowledgements

Writing this book would not have been possible had it not been for the inspiration, criticism and love of that select group of cherished individuals whom I will always regard as my true family and *autre coeur*: Barbara, Irene Bevan, René and Lucette Chevalier, Jacqueline Danno, Hélène Delavault, Marlene Dietrich, Tony Griffin, Renata and Gottfried Helnwein, Roger Normand, Betty Paillard, Annick Roux, Terry Sanderson, Monica Solash, John and Anne Taylor, and François and Madeleine Vals. God bless you all!

For sharing her private thoughts and reminiscences with me, but more so for being such a wonderful friend to Freddie in his greatest hour of need, my heart goes out to Montserrat Caballé. No man could have wished for a kinder, more understanding confidante.

I am also deeply indebted to Isabelle Caballé, David Evans, Jim Jenkins, Kurt, Michael, Mike Moran, Elaine Paige, Kate Weston and David Wigg.

Very special thanks to my agent, David Bolt, and *chapeau-bas* to a wonderful publishing team at Robson Books.

Particular thanks to Jackie Gunn and Val Moss of the

International Queen Fan Club, Hannie Roggeveen of the Official Dutch Queen Fan Club and Frieda Sarhadi of *The Royal Gazette*.

For their help and contribution to this book I also thank the following: Jason Barker, Iain Blair, Rusi Dalal, Andy Davis, Adrian Deevoy, Robin Denselow, Harry Doherty, Richard Ellis, Sharon Feinstein, John Gill, David Hancock, Tony Hicks, Bill Higgins, Jim Hutton, James Johnson, Henrietta Knight, Götz Kühnemund, Alain Lavanne, John Marshall, Geoff Mayfield, Richard Middleton, Kate Molly, Chris Morris, Jeff Moses, Mike Parker, Tony Parsons, Willie Pepper, Mark Putterford, David Quantick, Julianne Regan, Robert Sandall, Paul Scott, Jonathan Singer, Merrill Shindler, Richard Smith, Peter Stein, Tony Stewart, Andy Stout, Sally Stratton, Baudouin Struye, Phil Sutcliffe, Johnny Waller, Stephen Williams, Anthony Wood, Toby Young and the Principal of St Peter's School, Panchgani.

For graciously allowing me access to valuable features and interviews, I thank the editors and staff of the following publications past and present. The *Baghdad Observer*, *Billboard*, *Daily Express*, *Daily Mail*, *Daily Mirror*, *Daily Telegraph*, *Dayton Daily News*, *Gay Times*, *Guitarist*, *Guardian*, *Hard-Rock Français*, *Kerrang*, *London Evening Standard*, *London Press Service*, *Metal Hammer*, *More-Belgique*, *Music Express*, *Music & Media*, *New Musical Express*, *News of the World*, *New York Globe*, *Oxford Mail*, *People*, *Playgirl*, *Q*, *Record Collector*, *Record & Popswop Mirror*, *Rock-Circus*, *Rockline*, *RIP*, *RSVP*, *Sounds*, *Sun*, *Sunday Mirror*, *Sunday Times*, *Time Out*, *Today*, *Tracks*, *The Times*, and *Top 40*.

Most important of all, as in the best revues the best acts only come on at the end, I would like to express my thanks, *coeur et âme*, to Freddie Mercury, to Marleau Bret for inspiring me to write this book in the first place, and to my wife Jeanne who still is the keeper of my soul.

Foreword

Throughout Europe, and in America and Japan, wherever I sing I am still approached by Freddie Mercury's fans. They ask me what he was like to work with. They tell me how much they love him still, that when he died, part of them died with him.

Freddie's music and his qualities as a human being directly touched the hearts of his admirers, yet he is constantly cricitized and his life turned into a moral epic. No one person has the right to judge another person. Freddie lived his life without pretence, exactly the way he felt he should, and he should be respected for that. Even those finest examples of humanity – Gandhi and Mother Theresa of Calcutta – admitted that they had faults, and if *they* considered themselves imperfect in any way, who are we to judge a man who brought so much joy and goodness into the world?

I find it very moving to witness such devotion, yet I am not surprised because Freddie was a good, non-violent, peace-loving man who was generous not just to his friends and those he loved, but to others who suffered the way he did.

I will always remember Freddie as a good friend, an honest

and courageous man – especially towards the end of his life –
a man who was very, *very* special for thousands of people.
And you know, thousands of people cannot be wrong.

Montserrat Caballé,
Barcelona, August 1996

Introduction

> You can have everything in the world and still be the loneliest man – that is the most bitter type of loneliness. Success has brought me world idolization and millions of pounds, but it's prevented me from having the one thing we all need – a loving, on-going relationship.

This was Freddie Mercury – pop icon, showman, raconteur, diva, authority on the human condition, clown-prince and unquestionable genius – speaking in a rare interview with the *News of the World* in April 1985. The occasion commemorated the release of his first solo album, 'Mr Bad Guy', comprising eleven self-composed songs, several of which may retrospectively be regarded as portentous: *There Must Be More to Life Than This, Love Me Like There's No Tomorrow, My Love is Dangerous, Fooling Around* . . .

Friends and colleagues have readily maintained that Freddie's promiscuity – no different from that of the average pop star, regardless of sexual preference – was precipitated and fuelled by an abject loneliness stemming from a fragmented childhood which, though never lacking in love and affection, had seen him endure lengthy periods of separation from his family. 'My biggest nightmare has always been walking into an empty bedroom,' he admitted once, in a statement reminiscent of those final, torturous Judy Garland concerts in London when she had screamed, 'I don't wanna go home! What is there at home for me?' It was this crippling loneliness which prompted Freddie to say, after performing in front of 250,000 wildly adoring fans in Rio de Janeiro, 'I was the loneliest person there.'

His was the psyche most readily associated with those *monstres sacrées*, mostly female, who are so embroiled in their public personae – married to their audiences – that any kind of relationship, physical or otherwise, cannot be easily sustained while the legend persists. Yet persist it must, otherwise existence would be meaningless. The list is endless: Davis, Crawford, Piaf, Bankhead, Dietrich, Garbo – all greatly admired by Freddie Mercury, all searching for that crock of gold at the end of the rainbow, but only coming close to finding it in the spotlight's glare.

Like his *alter egos*, Freddie is to be commended for his honesty. When asked if he was homosexual, James Dean quipped, 'Well, I'm certainly not going through life with one hand tied behind my back!' Freddie's response to the same question, given to a journalist from the *New Musical Express*, was, 'I've had more lovers than Elizabeth Taylor. I've got a big bed which sleeps six. I'm as gay as a daffodil, my dear!' This was Freddie at his most flippant – the newspapers expected an outrageous reply and were never disappointed. A few years later, one could only detect the note of anguish in his voice when he confessed that love, for him, was like playing Russian roulette. He added, 'I try to hold back when I'm attracted to someone, but I just can't control love. It runs riot. All my one-night stands are just me playing my part.'

This was Freddie's essence, a Janus character who was equally at home telling the media that he was 'essentially a private man', never becoming a spokesman for the gay community, hardly ever expressing his views on contentious issues. On the other side of the coin, however, he was blatantly extroverted, rebellious, more outrageous than *any* of his contemporaries, and one of the most thrilling personalities of the last half of this century.

He was probably best summed up by John Marshall of *Gay Times*, whose lengthy, uncompromising eulogy in January 1992 served as a welcome antidote to the wealth of often pretentious and sometimes downright poisonous obituaries which had appeared in the British press.

He was a 'scene-queen', not afraid to publicly express his gayness but unwilling to analyse or justify his lifestyle . . . It was as if Freddie Mercury was saying to the world, 'I am what I am. So what?' And that in itself was a statement.

1

Looking to Find My Goal

He was born Faroukh Bulsara, at the Government Hospital on the small island of Zanzibar, off the coast of what was then Tanganyika, on 5 September 1946 – the eldest child of Bomi, an itinerant Persian clerk with the British government who with his wife Jer had set up home in Zanzibar, after leaving their native Bombay. The Bulsaras were Parsees – followers of Zoroaster, and direct descendants of those Persians who had fled to India in the seventh and eighth centuries to avoid Muslim persecution. They were not an inordinately wealthy family by any means though, in common with most colonials in the last years of the Raj, the Bulsaras did have a coterie of servants which catered for their every need – though there was *never* anyone there to fasten his shoelaces for him and wash his neck, as Freddie once joked.

When he was five, Faroukh was enrolled at the local missionary school. Soon afterwards, in 1952, his only sister, Kashmira, was born. Then, in 1954, Bomi was transferred back to Bombay, still in the same employ, but with a larger 'round' of high courts to visit. So that his education would not suffer – he was an alert, intelligent child – Bomi had his son enrolled at St Peter's, a prestigious English boarding-school at Panchgani, a hill-station some fifty miles from Bombay. The move coincided with him being ordained a fully fledged Parsee, partaking of the *Navjote*, or cleansing ritual, and reciting the sacred prayers of Zoroaster while donning the *sudreh* or traditional white muslin shirt of purity.

Freddie had never been really close to his father, largely on account of Bomi's lengthy absences from home. Now, in an utterly Etonesque environment, the Faroukh was rapidly dispensed with – for the rest of his short life he would be known only as Freddie, or by intimate gay friends such as Elton John, as Melina after the famous Greek actress, Melina Mercouri, who herself told me years later that some of *her* close friends had called her Freddie! He also adapted readily to the school's Spartan discipline, reflecting, 'You *had* to do as you were told, so the most sensible thing was to make the best of it. I learned how to look after myself, and I grew up very quickly.'

In keeping with colonial tradition, St Peter's School followed a typically 'gung-ho' sporting calendar: rugby, cricket, football, boxing, table tennis and athletics. Freddie loathed cricket and most track events – according to one school pal, 'scurrying down the track like a demented Jerry Lewis'. With equal fervour, he adored boxing and table tennis, becoming school champion by the age of ten. In later years there would often be a table in a corner of the recording studio, and to give his opponent a chance against his exceptional skills he would always play left-handed, with the other hand behind his back. He was also efficient at English, though his true forte was art, a medium which nevertheless found him at his most frenetic. Friends have testified that in these early days, though the enthusiasm and talent were undoubtedly there, patience was not one of Freddie's finer virtues and he hardly ever completed a picture or drawing. Like many boys, he collected postage stamps. The collection he amassed was not particularly large, but it did contain many important early items from Zanzibar, and many years later his 'Blue Album' would be sold for thousands of pounds and the money donated to charity.

Another important element in his development was Freddie's interest in music, particularly in the recordings of the playback singer, Lata Mangeshkar, then as now India's top entertainer. Born in 1929 and known as 'The Nightingale of India', this fascinating performer had been the favourite of the country's first prime minister, Pandit Nehru. She performed in twenty languages, including Sanskrit and Hindi, and had a vast repertoire of 30,000 songs. The very first concert Freddie attended, in November 1959, was a gala performance by Mangeshkar in Bombay, and the sheer power of her voice and her range of material so fascinated him that he saw her again in Poona, and in Panchgani in 1961, when she paid a visit to St Peter's to sing at their summer fête. Mangeshkar and several others have since maintained that Freddie would have made a fine playback singer, though with his vibrant personality and love of showing off, it is doubtful he would have ever been satisfied to limit himself to mere film soundtracks.

The library at St Peter's housed an extensive collection of Lata Mangeshkar records, many albums by the equally legendary Egyptian singer Oum Kalthoum, whom he also frequently impersonated, and a good many more be-bop, twist, Cliff Richard and Tommy Steele records sent over from England. Freddie played anything he could get his hands on – all were instrumental in forging his future.

Amateur dramatics, too, were an important part of Freddie's curriculum, and because it was an all-male environment, St Peter's had long-since adopted Shakespeare's own tradition that female roles be played by boys. Freddie considered that this was going a little *too* far, though from his early teens he was well aware of the 'camp' aspect of dramatization because of his admiration for Gielgud and Olivier, whose over-the-top film portrayals of the bard's heroes were shown regularly at the school. Like all public schools, too, St Peter's had its clandestine coterie of homosexuals with whom Freddie felt perfectly comfortable once he became aware of his own sexuality – mindless of the fact that sex outside marriage, let alone with a member of one's own gender, was fiercely condemned by the Parsee community.

Freddie's first love affair – if it could be deemed as such – occurred during the spring of 1961, when he was fourteen. It was with a seventeen-year-old youth nicknamed 'the Master' on account of his quintessentially English though snooty Noël Coward mannerisms. 'I had a crush on the Master, and would have done *anything* for him,' Freddie later admitted. 'Going to bed with him didn't feel wrong, and though I'd never made love with a woman, I asked myself if *that* would be worth all the fuss!'

In fact, there was much more to it than this. The Master – his actual name was Robert – was an overweight, unattractive and by all accounts thoroughly unpleasant individual who took advantage of Freddie's slight physique and timidity by bullying him into having a relationship with him. One of Freddie's classmates, who still lives in Panchgani and who asked to be identified only as Michael, recounted Freddie's own story of how he had lost his virginity to this young man:

Several of Freddie's pals, myself included, knew that we were gay from quite early on, but we were terrified to do anything about it. The consequences of being caught out in those days were horrendous, so instead of actually doing anything, we would get our kicks from spying on the older boys whilst they were bathing. Unfortunately,

Freddie was nabbed by the Master and carted off to the gardener's shed where he was knocked about a bit and forced to have sex with him. Freddie told me about it a couple of weeks later, but when I asked him why he hadn't reported the matter to the Principal, he said that it was because he'd enjoyed the experience so much. Later, of course, he told me that he'd only stuck with the Master because he'd been petrified of admitting his feelings to anyone else in case he ended up being sent down. What also struck me as strange, certainly at that time, was the fact that on account of the Master, poor Freddie assumed that S and M and homosexuality went hand in glove. Then, after the summer term the Master returned to England to live with his family, and Freddie fell head-over-heels in love with a beautiful Indian boy who worked in the gardens. His name was Sanjay, he was twenty-three, and he and Freddie spent as much time together as they could, mostly at weekends, until Freddie left the school.

Meanwhile, encouraging him in his artistic interests, Freddie's father consented to an increase in his allowance so that he could take up a musical instrument. Freddie chose the piano, substituted Mangeshkar for Mozart, and within the space of a few years had passed his Grade IV Theory and Practical. He joined the school's choir, which though multicultural was compelled to perform traditional Christian hymns, Handel, Bach, and even Gregorian chants and Jewish *cheseds*. More importantly for Freddie, with a group of friends and despite his intense shyness, he formed his first band, the Hectics, which, though only allowed to perform at in-house functions, fared reasonably well.

Freddie, strange to say in view of his later exhibitionism, was not the Hectics' frontman – this honour went to a youngster named Bruce Murray. In 1962, however, this somewhat idyllic existence was brought to a halt when

Freddie sat his 'O' levels. Achieving good results in English Language, History, Art and Music, he announced that he had had enough of school and a few weeks later – bidding his beloved Sanjay goodbye – he returned to his family in Zanzibar.

The island protectorate was about to enter a period of political turmoil as it battled towards Independence from the British. The first round of elections took place towards the end of 1963 – when most experts expected the Africans who formed the majority of the population to win. They did not, succumbing to the Arab minority in this and the next two polls until, on 10 December 1963, Zanzibar broke free of British rule. One month later it merged with Tanganyika to form Tanzania, causing the Africans to mount an unsuccessful insurrection which nevertheless forced the flight of thousands of Britons and Indians. The Bulsaras, cramming what belongings they could into a few suitcases, headed for England.

For a while they stayed with relatives in Feltham, Middlesex, before purchasing a modest semi in the area. Bomi then took a job as an accountant with the Trust House Forté group, while Freddie enrolled on a course with Isleworth Polytechnic – it was essential that he gain his Art 'A' level to ensure a place at college. His parents were opposed to the idea. Like a great many colonials, they tended to frown upon the artistic milieu, and had probably hoped that Freddie might follow in his father's footsteps. Also, while the Bulsaras shunned the British society they had been forcibly ejected into, retreating into the tiny Parsee community, Freddie greedily lapped up this exciting new world of 'Swinging Sixties' London. For a time, according to Rusi Dalal, who had grown up with Freddie in Zanzibar, he would drop by at the Parsee Temple in West Hampstead, but as these visits decreased he distanced himself more and more from his parents eventually moving out of their house into a tiny flat in Kensington, at the time the centre of activity for the 'in crowd'.

In his spare time and during the holidays, Freddie supported himself with a variety of *ad hoc* jobs. He washed pots in the kitchens at Heathrow airport, and stacked crates at a warehouse on the Feltham Industrial Estate. Here, he was ribbed by some of the rough and ready factory-hands on account of his unusual colouring, protruding front teeth, posh accent and effeminate mannerisms, though he soon won everyone over with his ready charm and knack of self-parody. 'Nobody could take the piss out of me as much as I could take the piss out of myself,' he later said.

At the end of his college course, in April 1966, Freddie's hard work was rewarded with a Grade A pass in Art, and he was accepted for a course in graphic design by Ealing College of Art. For Freddie, this was a double celebration – Ealing's former students included Peter Townshend, who had formed The Who there, and the Small Faces' Ronnie Wood, later of the Rolling Stones.

Freddie's consuming passion at college was Jimi Hendrix, the hard-living, drug-addicted rock star from Seattle. He executed dozens of paintings and drawings of his idol, which he framed and hung on the walls of his flat. On occasions he would ape Hendrix in class, ruffling his hair and strumming away on an imaginary guitar – a 12-inch ruler – while belting out *Purple Haze*.

Freddie's closest friend at Ealing was Tim Staffell, already a pop 'veteran'. In 1964, with three fellow pupils from Hampton Grammar School, vocalist Staffell had formed the futuristic group 1984, which had been augmented by a Feltham guitarist named Brian May. Aided by his father, May had built his soon-to-be-legendary 'Red Special' guitar, to his own specification for just £8 using bits and bobs from around the house, an antique fire-surround for the neck and his mother's pearl buttons for fret-markers. The group had split in 1967, though May and Staffell – the former enrolling on an Astro-physics course at Imperial College – had remained close and quickly set about forming another group. May had placed an advertisement on his college noticeboard: WANTED; GINGER BAKER TYPE DRUMMER.

The pair had settled on Roger Taylor, an eighteen-year-old dentistry student, Norfolk-born, but for many years a resident of Truro, in Cornwall. The group was Smile, which on 28 October made a prestigious enough début at Imperial College supporting Pink Floyd. As a matter of course, Tim Staffell introduced Freddie to the band, and Brian May was amazed that, though they only lived around the corner from each other, he and Freddie had never met. Freddie was then invited to accompany Smile on the college circuit, where they attracted a modest following playing mostly cover-versions of other groups' hits, and the occasional original composition. Later, Smile supported Yes and T Rex, and in February 1969 appeared at the Royal Albert Hall in a charity concert for unmarried mothers. It was hosted by John Peel, and part of it still survives on film. The line-up included such luminaries as Free, Joe Cocker and the Bonzo Dog Doo Dah Band.

In June 1969 Smile cut their first single at Trident Studios for the American Mercury label – *Earth*, penned by Tim Staffell, coupled with his and Brian May's *Step On Me*. Unfortunately the recording was only issued in the United States, with hardly any airplay and no support from the record company. It flopped, and the group's other songs for Mercury fell by the wayside because the company had no base in Britain and therefore no contractual rights to release them on home ground. *Blag*, *Polar Bear* and *April Lady* resurfaced early in 1994 on a bootleg CD, 'The Unobtainable Royal Chronicle'. In the spring of 1970, however, Tim Staffell would leave the group, and after an unsuccessful venture with another outfit, Humpy Bong, he gave up his musical career to concentrate on television special effects. A few years later he worked on the models for *Thomas the Tank Engine*.

Freddie's preoccupation, having witnessed the students'

enthusiasm for Smile, was to front a band of his own. He was also desperately unhappy with his home life. His father was virulently opposed to him embarking precociously on a showbiz career, and there were so many arguments with Bomi that Freddie would often stay away from the Feltham house for days and even weeks at a time. Sometimes he would crash down at Roger Taylor's flat in Sinclair Road, or more often than not spend the night with two other student friends, Chris Smith and Paul Humberstone, who shared a flat in Kensington's Addison Gardens.

With his natural charm, wit and infectious personality, Freddie was an all-round favourite, though his aspirations towards greatness must have been a little wearing at times. Chris Smith, who played briefly with Smile and collaborated with Freddie on some of his earliest songs, remembered how the flamboyant youth had once stood up in a packed London pub and yelled, 'I'm not going to be a star. I'm going to be a *legend*!' Tim Staffell recalled:

> Freddie was *already* a star at college. He exuded confidence in everything he did and was committed to becoming famous. Some people poked fun at him, but he always floored them with a witty response. Freddie developed this camp side of his nature, but at no time was it ever suggested that he was gay. He was never *overtly* sexual.

In spite of his burning ambition, however, like Brian May and Roger Taylor, Freddie was sensible enough to realize that many such pipe-dreams never pay off. For this reason, he heeded his father's advice, and like them continued with his studies. May and Taylor gained their respective B.Sc.s, and Freddie left Ealing in the summer of 1969 with a Diploma in Graphic Art and Design.

For a little while Freddie tried looking for a job, and through a family friend received a handful of commissions –

one was to draw a series of advertisements for lingerie and corsets. The lure of the stage, however, was overpowering, and ignoring his father's pleas he began searching for something that *he* wanted to do.

Thinking that his classical training might give his college chums the impression that he was too snooty, he purchased a second-hand guitar and a set of textbooks, then went about learning the basic chords and began working on his first compositions – not an easy task, for in those formative years someone had to be close at hand to write down the notes. 'I was learning a lot of things about song structure,' he later reflected. 'As for lyrics, I found *them* quite a task. My strongest point was melody content. I concentrated on this, and the lyrics came afterwards.'

Freddie became actively involved with Ibex, a Liverpud-lian group newly arrived in London, who were hoping to make their mark on the college circuit. Ibex comprised Mike Bersin on guitar, Mick 'Miffer' Smith on drums and John 'Tupp' Taylor on bass. All were in their late teens, and they first met Freddie in his and Smile's local pub, the Kensington.

Because none of the trio considered himself a competent vocalist, they reluctantly decided to audition Freddie, whose cod-opera-vocalese improvisations during some of Smile's gigs had not gone unnoticed after he had heckled them for being 'bland and undemonstrative'. He was hired on the spot, mindless of the fact that the others in the group had found his camp demeanour slightly offputting. This campness, of course, would be turned by him into an art form and become an integral component of his stage persona, without which his future projects would not have been quite so magical.

While he was getting to grips with Ibex, Freddie supplemented his income by setting up a business venture with Roger Taylor selling bric-à-brac, paintings, quality second-hand clothes, fur coats and the like in Kensington Market's 'Death Row' – thus named because of its wealth of antique stalls. Freddie was in his element, and in his outlandish garb complemented by multicoloured silk scarves, wide-brimmed hats, feather boas and black-lacquered fingernails fitted in well with the in-crowd. He and Taylor did not make a lot of money, just enough to see them through from one week to the next and to pay for Freddie's 'little foibles', such as his insistence on travelling virtually everywhere by taxi. 'He always looked and acted like a star, though he was penniless,' Brian May recalled. 'He would bring home great bags of stuff, pull out a strip of something and say, "Look at this beautiful garment, it's going to fetch a fortune!" And I'd say, "Fred, it's a piece of *rag*!"'

With Ibex, and *never* in style – the mode of transport was an old Transit van, borrowed from a friend – Freddie travelled up and down England, working clubs and pubs. In the north there was frequent prejudice on account of the area's homophobia, more often than not incurred by the group's strange appearance. Spray-on satin trousers, velvet and lace shirts, gold-lamé capes and a wealth of plumes were too much for staid, macho environments such as Rochdale and Oldham, though, in common with many camp entertainers – Liberace, Danny La Rue, Johnnie Ray – Freddie was a great favourite with 'Bingo Lils' and middle-aged matrons, who only wanted to mother him. 'Roger (Taylor) and I go poncing and ultrablagging just about everywhere,' Freddie wrote to a close friend, Celine Daley, at the end of October from the flat he was now sharing with Smile, in Barnes. 'Lately we're being termed as a couple of queens. Which reminds me that Miffer the sod went and told everybody down here that I had seriously turned into a fully fledged queer.' And if Freddie's friends from these years, in trying to protect his name, have insisted sometimes quite fervently that they saw no evidence of his having homosexual tendencies, Smith's comments were supported many years later by an admission from Mike Bersin to Andy Davis of *Record Collector*, 'He was kind of straight then. But if he hadn't yet come out of the closet, he was certainly looking through the keyhole.'

Freddie's first professional appearance took place on 23 August 1969, during an afternoon 'bluesology' matinée at Bolton's Octagon Theatre – an event for which no one was paid other than travelling expenses, but to which scores of minor impresarios and working-men's club concert secretaries had been invited. The advertising for these shows stated that any artist or group worthy of their name would be assured of walking off with a clutch of bookings. More often than not, however, the organizers were only after a free show.

Ibex opened their set with *Lover*, a song written by Freddie and Mike Bersin which would reappear, some years later with some of its original lines intact, as *Liar*, on Queen's début album. Performing this, Freddie effortlessly managed to make himself stand out from everyone else on the bill. Ibex's road-manager, Ken Testi, later recalled, 'Everything he did on stage later in Queen, he was doing with Ibex . . . marching from one end of the stage to another, from left to right and back again. Stomping about. He brought dynamics, freshness and presentation to the band that had been completely lacking, previously.' And now, without even bothering to ask his name, a photographer from the *Bolton Evening News* took several shots of Freddie – his first ever during a public performance – one of which appeared with the caption, 'One of the performers gets into his stride.'

But even if Freddie appeared to be having fun, he was very much out of his depth in this part of the world. The crunch came after Ibex's time in Liverpool, where they played the Sink Club, a tiny establishment in the basement of the Rumbling Tum, a seedy greasy-spoon in Hardman Street.

It has recently emerged that part of their set – a half-hour compilation of Beatles, Hendrix, Cream and Led Zeppelin songs – was taped by Geoff Higgins, the group's driver, though as yet it has not been released commercially. It is also known that Smile too were playing in Liverpool that night, at the Green Door, and that after their performance they turned up at the Sink Club just in time to join Freddie and his friends on the stage . . . and just as Higgins's tape was running out, robbing the world of what was effectively Queen's début performance, albeit in an unorthodox fashion.

Freddie found Liverpool so unpleasant – particularly one evening when he was accosted by a gang of drunken skinheads – that he rushed back to London and very nearly threw in the towel. Within days, however, he had bounced back with a brainwave – Ibex had been an unlucky name, so henceforth his outfit would be known as Wreckage. And to prove a point, he personally spray-painted the new name on their instruments and gear.

This move coincided with the departure of the apparently homophobic Mick 'Miffer' Smith. Freddie commented in his letter to Celine Daley, 'Miffer's not with us any more . . . the bastard just up and left one morning saying he was going to be a milkman back in Widnes.' Smith was replaced with Richard Thompson, the former drummer with 1984.

Wreckage played their first gig at Ealing College on 31 October 1969 – the sole evidence of which is one of the fly-posters and a hastily typed setlist which was auctioned by Sotheby's during the summer of 1996. The group supported Iron Butterfly at Imperial College on 5 November, and at several rugby clubs, before staging their farewell concert at the Wade Dean Grammar School for Girls, where 'Tupp' Taylor's sister was a pupil, just after Christmas.

Over the next few weeks, Freddie scoured the music press for audition notices. One, in *Melody Maker*, was for a vocalist with a four-piece blues band, Sour Milk Sea, and took place in Leatherhead, Surrey, on 6 February 1970. Accompanying him for moral support were Roger Taylor and John Harris, Smile's road-manager. Looking like a turn-of-the-century roué in his tightest crimson crushed velvet trousers, boots and fox fur, Freddie breezed into the audition room – a church crypt! – with such panache that he was engaged without anyone showing much interest in what he sounded like.

Sour Milk Sea, so named after the George Harrison song, had been formed in 1968 by ex-public schoolboy Chris Dummett (later Chris Chesney). Very soon Freddie was boasting that he and Dummett were lovers, especially after the pair moved into Smile's flat. 'I had a good relationship with Freddie,' Dummett confessed some years later, though he denied that they had an actual affair. 'We were like Bowie and Ronson, where we related physically to each other on stage.'

Shortly afterwards, Sour Milk Sea played their only important date, a charity gig for Shelter, at Highfield Parish Hall, Headington, on 20 March, when Dummett told Anthony Wood of the *Oxford Mail*, 'I don't feel we are like any other group. Our approach is based on our relationships with one another.' Once again it was Freddie who stole the limelight, as the only one of the group directly facing the camera for their 'publicity shot', which appeared alongside Wood's feature. Needless to say, such favouritism and innocuous narcissism caused friction – and fisticuffs – among the members of Sour Milk Sea. After a handful of further engagements, the outfit folded. So too ended Freddie's friendship with Chris Dummett . . . a series of events which happened to coincide with Smile's demise.

The trio of May, Taylor and Bulsara were living under the same roof, sharing the same financial hardships and nurturing exactly the same ideas – it was inevitable, therefore, that their best and perhaps only option for success depended upon each other and the combining of their respective, obvious talents. This done, in April 1970 they set about choosing a marketable name for their outfit. May and Taylor drew up a shortlist of two names: Grand Dance, and Rich Kids. Freddie favoured neither, declaring the second choice somewhat pretentious, and insisted upon Queen – a name which, with its double connotation of camp and grandeur, in this new era of glam-rock, could hardly have been more appropriate.

'We prefer to think of Queen in the regal sense rather than in the queer one,' was how Freddie was still apparently defending his choice, three years later to a stuffy American journalist. 'We never copied *anyone*. Our way was putting together a different kind of theatrical music. Bowie was already doing glam-rock. We *want* to be dandy, we *want* to be shocking and outrageous so that people will *know* whether they like us or not the moment they see us!' May and Taylor offered a weak, futile argument. Such a name was too strong. It might even make them a laughing-stock! Freddie was adamant, however, relying on a mixture of intuition and the precognitive dream – the fact that all *will* turn out well in the end, so long as this is what one wishes.

Queen it was!

For Queen, the next six months were a sometimes arduous trail of trial and error – auditioning no less than six successive bass-players, not one of whom matched up to the verve and dazzling personality of the group's key figure. The first was Mike Grose, Roger Taylor's pal from St Austell. Grose was particularly useful because he owned a van and some PA equipment – which the other three could not yet afford – and he thought nothing of leaving his own band, Bent Cement, and trekking up to London to attend the rehearsals which Brian May had organized in an empty lecture hall at Imperial College. The songs, written by May and Freddie, were mostly rehashes of the material they had supplied for Smile and Ibex, and it was with these that they proposed their first concert.

Before this happened, however, Freddie changed his name – something he had been wanting to do for some time, not just for the sake of his career but to shrug off the shackles of his colonial past and prove to any detractors, most especially

his parents and the stuffy members of the tightly knit Parsee
community, that here was a force to be reckoned with.
Mercury, the Roman god of skill and eloquence, was the
ruling planet of his birthsign, Virgo, *and* the messenger of the
gods. A name which would serve him well.

This metamorphosis really did enable Freddie to obliterate
his past. His close friend David Evans, of whom more later,
told me:

> Faroukh Bulsara was a name he had buried. He never
> wanted to talk about any period in his life *before* he
> became Freddie Mercury, and everything about Freddie
> Mercury was a self-constructed thing. Like Marlene
> Dietrich he was a strange double personality – like a
> rose grafted on to common stock. If you have a strong
> enough common stock, it will support the wonderful
> creature you have created. If it's rotten stock, then the
> whole thing will collapse.

Several weeks before their split, Smile had been booked by
Roger Taylor's mother for a gig at Truro City Hall in aid of
the Red Cross. This still took place on 27 July 1970, and
though the newspaper advertisements billed them as Smile,
the public were effectively seeing Queen – or at least
three-quarters of them – for the first time. They opened with
Wreckage's *Stone Cold Crazy*, and the largely rural audience
did not quite know what to make of what one journalist
described as, 'Four very peculiar-looking young gentlemen
clad in silk and too many jewels, making enough row to
wake half the dead in Cornwall'. Their reception was much
warmer a few weeks later, however, when they played
Imperial College – the audience was made up mostly of their
friends and former classmates. Even so, at the end of July
they returned to Cornwall for another gig – and while there
parted company with Mike Grose, who since his arrival in
London had persistently complained of being homesick.

Grose was replaced by another of Roger Taylor's Cornish friends, Barry Mitchell, who played several small venues with them over the next few months – in and around London, and once travelling to Liverpool, which Freddie found more rewarding than his last trip. On 18 September there was a 'day of mourning' when, not unexpectedly, Jimi Hendrix died of a drugs-overdose, ending the career of the man whom many had fêted as the greatest guitarist of the decade. As a mark of respect, Freddie and Roger closed their market stall for the day. Also at around this time, tired of 'slumming it' by sharing accommodation with anyone who happened to be in the neighbourhood, the pair rented a larger flat at 100 Holland Road, in Shepherd's Bush. They were delighted to find a grand piano sitting in the living-room when they moved in – the previous tenant had left it there, unable to get it out of the room!

Early in January 1971, having played with them at the London Marquee and Ewell Technical College, in Surrey, Barry Mitchell more or less left the group in the lurch – although still performing to smallish audiences and earning little over expenses, Queen's diary over the next few months was looking decidedly healthy. Then, just as they were probably thinking they would never have an efficient line-up, Brian May and Roger Taylor were at a college disco when a friend introduced them to John Deacon, a nineteen-year-old Leicester-born bass player and student at Chelsea College who had seen Queen at a Kensington gig the previous October – and *not* been impressed! Now, he was invited to an audition at Imperial College, where he joined in with Freddie's and May's *Son and Daughter*, much to everyone's satisfaction. Thus, by the end of February 1971, Queen were ready for action.

2

Pagan Features . . .
Godlike Creatures

When college closed for its summer term, Queen headed off on another tour of Cornwall – organized by Roger, whose mother had found them a tiny cottage to rent, just outside Truro. Taking most of the credit for the venture, he cheekily billed them as 'The Legendary Drummer of Cornwall, Roger Taylor, and Queen' – the 'Queen' printed on playbills in letters smaller than those of his own name. The group fared reasonably well – after the usual pubs and clubs, the tour closed with their first open-air gig at the Tregye Country Club, where they were eighth on a bill of nine. Even so, when they returned to London in the September all four of them still had their feet very firmly on the ground. Still waiting for someone to convince them that they would make enough money to turn professional, Brian and John resumed their studies, and later took teaching jobs, while Roger did a volte-face, dropping dentistry to enrol on a course for a degree in biology with the North London Polytechnic. This meant that he had to give up working on his market stall, handing over the reins to Freddie, who shared the running of his business with another stall-holder, Alan Mair.

Queen's biggest break so far occurred early in 1972 when, having recorded a number of demos in the De Lane Lea Studios in Wembley – they were given a job setting up and testing the PA equipment, in return for what they readily assumed would be unlimited studio sessions for themselves – they were heard by Norman Sheffield, an executive from Trident Studios, the company who had earlier signed Smile. Sheffield was overwhelmed by the progress Roger and Brian had made in their playing techniques since then, and he was absolutely bowled over by Freddie's vocal brilliance and the overall quality of the band's demo tape, though it still needed a lot of work done on it. Agreeing to take them on, he persuaded Trident to supply Queen with the PA system they so desperately needed, and to allow them the use of his best studio to rehearse and record the songs for their début album. And still the boys refused to let the notion of success go to their heads. In June, John graduated with a first-class honours degree in electronics, and, unwilling to commit himself to a full-time career in music, immediately signed for a course which would hopefully gain him his M.Sc. A few weeks later Roger was awarded his biology degree.

Because the group were compelled to work in studio 'down-time' – in other words, when the studio was not being used by someone else, often at weekends or in the middle of the night – they spent many hours hanging around corridors and reception rooms, time which they put to good use composing and exchanging ideas. One afternoon Freddie was introduced to a producer, Robin Cable, who had been in the same studio a few weeks earlier when Phil and Ronnie Spector had been working there.

Cable nurtured two obsessions – the Beach Boys and the

famous Spector sound of the Sixties – which he now
combined by proposing that Freddie record the former's *I
Can Hear Music* in the very distinctive musical style of the
latter. The song was taped in a single take, but as Freddie
was not satisfied with the overall result – he disliked the
synthesizer interlude and the lack of percussion – Brian was
brought in to play a guitar harmony, and Roger to enhance it
with drums, castanets and tambourine. Freddie then
recorded, without the other two, his own arrangement of the
old Dusty Springfield hit *Goin' Back*. Cable took the tape
away and everyone forgot about it until the following year,
when EMI released the songs on a single. By this time Queen
were about to release their début album, so Freddie opted for
the pseudonym Larry Lurex. 'My own personal piss-take on
Gary Glitter,' he pronounced. Because of this, however, it
received little airplay, much criticism from Glitter's fans, and
was an unmitigated flop. Currently it is one of the most
elusive – and costly – items in the Queen back-catalogue.

Until then the group had remained unsalaried and virtually
on the breadline – doubly frustrating for the usually prudent
Brian May, who had turned down a research post at the
Jodrell Bank Observatory. Then, in mid-September, after
much discussion and argument, Trident awarded them the
somewhat shabby sum of £80 a week which, they were
forced to agree, was at least better than nothing. Two
months later they signed an agreement with the company:
Queen would record for Trident, who hopefully would
secure them the best possible deal with a reputable record
company.

To promote their latest acquisition – they already had
Bowie and Elton John, and Carly Simon would follow –
Trident organized a gig at the Pheasantry, a large club in
Chelsea. This took place on 6 November, and the evening
was a disaster. The PA system did not arrive until one hour
before the performance, and several invited dignitaries from
the recording world did not arrive at all. Much better was

their gig on 20 December at the Marquee, where, besides the songs on their imminent album, Queen set a precedent by performing Elvis Presley's *Jailhouse Rock*.

Queen's success at the Marquee led to them working more gigs than ever before, and for more money, though they were by no means in the same earnings bracket as many of the other bands on the local circuit. Even so, Roger was able to afford to move out of Freddie's flat into a place of his own in Richmond.

Although they would never be less than the best of friends, the move was welcomed by Freddie. Over the previous two years he had grown increasingly close to an ex-date of Brian's, Mary Austin, who was the nineteen-year-old manageress of the Biba boutique, one of the last bastions of the Swinging Sixties, then in Kensington Church Street, not far from Freddie's market stall.

In the last quarter-century there has been considerable speculation as to the actual nature of their relationship, much of it the result of Freddie's outspoken comments to the press. If the tabloids were looking for a spicy story he sure as hell would not disappoint them! This is unimportant, of course. Pretty, blonde, intellectual, calm and collected, Mary moved in with Freddie to become – and remain – not just his closest friend but his soul-mate and confidante. It was Mary who advised him on the all-important issues of make-up and fashion, on and off the stage. It was she who stood by him through his every joy and sorrow, success and crisis – even death itself. *That* is important.

Queen's album had been completed by the end of November, and approved by Trident, though there was still a little work to be done on the tracks, editing and mixing, and removing one or two gremlins which had got on to the tape which effectively meant it was not heard by any record company until early in the New Year. Following several rejections, it was taken to the MIDEM Festival in Cannes, by Trident's representative Ronnie Beck. Here, said to have been the only outstanding item in a very poor catalogue, it was accepted by Roy Featherstone of EMI – one of the companies who had rejected it in the first place.

Meanwhile, to prove their worth with the general public, as opposed to an audience of rowdy local drinkers who most of the time just happened to be where Queen were playing, this time the group were invited to participate in Radio One's 'Sounds of the Seventies' series – unpaid, though the potential from publicity was enormous. They recorded four songs at the Maida Vale Studios on 5 February 1973, and these were broadcast ten days later: Brian May's revamped version of his and Tim Staffell's *Doin' Alright*, his *Keep Yourself Alive*, and Freddie's evocative *Liar* and *My Fairy King* (all produced by Bernie Andrews). Immediately after the broadcast the BBC switchboard was jammed with calls from hundreds of listeners wanting to know more about Queen. A few weeks later the group signed a contract with EMI for Britain and Europe.

What fascinated everyone, of course, was Freddie's voice, with its unusually wide range – escalating within a few bars from a deep, throaty rock-growl to tender, vibrant tenor, then on to a high-pitched, almost perfect coloratura, pure and crystalline in the upper reaches. His highest recorded note, when he was almost forty and his vocal powers were at their peak, would be E above Top C . . . a phenomenon achieved outside opera only by Yma Sumac and Gracie Fields, and of which he once said, 'I use the Demis Roussos method. You get a pair of pliers under the frock, and you go *crunch*!' Like Barbra Streisand, too, he could cram an astonishing number of words into the briefest bar – *Stone Cold Crazy* is a prime example – and still retain perfect diction. Like Piaf he could produce a sob, if the ambience called for it.

On 9 April Queen returned to the Marquee. The occasion was a showcase aimed at pleasing Jack Holsen, the managing director of Elektra, the company which would be putting out their records in the United States, providing of course Holsen liked what he saw. His decision could not have been made any easier by the large number of empty seats – once again, most of the invited audience had shunned the event, having been forewarned by certain sections of the music press that this was just another hype from EMI.

Wearing a black-spangled, skin-tight catsuit, and with the fingernails of one silver-chainmailed hand lacquered black, a pencil-slim Freddie was played on to the stage by Brian May's recently composed instrumental overture, *Procession* – which Queen had decided to use as an opener for their next album, such was their confidence in their abilities. Preening himself in front of the drum-kit, Freddie minced audaciously from one side of the stage to the other, pausing only to pout or thrust his crotch at the amazed audience in a masterpiece of combined exhibitionism and buffoonery which only he was capable of getting away with and still be taken seriously.

A few days later the first reviews of the gig appeared in the music press, a mixed bag of praise and condemnation. The group were alternatively, 'A bunch of raving poofters trying to jump on to the Bowie bandwagon while doing a poor piss-take of Black Sabbath', and, 'Quite simply breathtaking. *The* band of the future!' Whatever these rags said was, however, of little consequence to Jack Holsen – he had already given Queen the thumbs-up.

Queen's first single, Brian's *Keep Yourself Alive*, c/w his *Son and Daughter*, was released by EMI on 6 July 1973. Against company policy, the group had chosen the songs, setting what would be for the next three decades a precedent deciding what would or would not end up on record-shop shelves. The finicky, prejudiced music press by and large disliked it for no apparent reason (it is now known) than that it was different, superior to much of the dross in the pop charts it failed to reach, through lack of air-play. *Melody Maker* even had the audacity to admonish, 'Do us *all* a favour, fellas. Change your name to the Uncouth and go on

stage in jock-straps!' Only the *New Musical Express*, whose
representative had not been at the Marquee, gave them the
credit they deserved, declaring, 'If these guys look *half* as good
as they sound, they could be huge!'

In anticipation of the group's success, and never one to do
things by halves, Freddie had designed their logo, plumping
after some consideration for a family crest devised from their
birthsigns. For Roger and John, both Leo, there were two
lions-rampant flanking the large, crown-enclosed Q, capped
by a Cancerian crab (Brian), the whole surmounted by a large
phoenix, the symbol of hope and renewed youth. Below the
lions, and a deliberate pun, were two small fairies which
Freddie said represented his own sign – Virgo.

The début album, entitled simply 'Queen', was released on
13 July. Produced by John Anthony and Ray Thomas Baker, it
had a superb cover photograph by Doug Puddifoot, a friend of
Roger's who had covered the group's Cornish tour and taken
some interesting shots of Smile. Freddie was depicted in his
soon-to-be-classic pose, arms outstretched for an encore,
holding aloft the microphone stand, silhouetted from behind
by two large, powerful spotlights. In Britain, initially at least,
the album was not a resounding success – according to most
authorities, because it should have been released to coincide
with the Marquee showcase, not three months afterwards. In
America, however, it sold very well, prompting a New York
journalist to fly at once to London to interview the group.
'Queen should be giving glam-rockers like Bowie and the
Sweet a run for their money,' Jonathan Singer proclaimed in
Circus, concluding coyly, 'With one added attraction –
musicianship!'

Throughout the interview, Freddie fidgeted a lot or used his
cuff to polish the spangles on his catsuit, and expressed some
concern for Queen's future:

We still worry that the name Queen will give people the
wrong idea. We want to be a good British regal rock

band, and we'll stick to that way of thinking. Our music should override the image because we'll concentrate on putting out good product the whole time. We might get a bit of a pop-tag, but it won't last. We're confident people will take to us because, although the camp image has already been established by Bowie and Bolan, we're taking it to another level.

It was a supreme example of inefficient publicity which inadvertently gave Queen a big break. The copy of the album sent to Mike Appleton, the producer of BBC2's legendary rock programme, 'The Old Grey Whistle Test', had neither label nor publicity handout. Thus, not knowing who or what he was playing, but impressed all the same – he later swore that he had not heard the single – Appleton included it in the programme which went out on 24 July, over a piece of animated documentary footage of Franklin D Roosevelt's wartime presidential election campaign. Needless to say, the programme received a number of urgent calls – including an irate one from a Trident executive – and the next day Queen found themselves whisked off to the BBC to tape four songs for Radio One's top-rating showcase, 'The John Peel Show'. Besides the two songs from the single, they re-recorded *Liar* from the album, and a new song, *See What a Fool I've Been*.

A few days later the quartet began working on a short film at Shepperton Studios, commissioned by Trident to promote their album in Europe and the United States – 'Queen' was to be released there on 4 September. Freddie, who had been told by the director Mike Mansfield to think up a marketable gimmick, as usual went over the top – he shaved his chest! Filming was an unpleasant, unnatural experience for them all. For one thing, they had never mimed before, and grew very frustrated during *Liar* when the tempo rose and it was almost impossible to keep in synch while the cameramen were constantly bumping into them in their attempts to film from as many awkward angles as possible. Also, the sets were white when Freddie had emphasized they should be black – a 'truc' often used on the continent by contemporaries Johnny Halliday and Eddie Mitchell. After a few tantrums from both sides, Mansfield was shown the door and, directed by Queen themselves – yet another precedent – the project was completed the way they wanted it. Trident then assigned them their first publicist, Tony Brainsby, who had worked with such diverse acts as Cat Stevens, Paul McCartney and Mott The Hoople.

Queen were now working hard on their second album, 'Queen II', though at their own pace now that Trident had given them their own studio . . . and issued a press statement to the effect that the group would have to make it because they had already set Trident back in excess of £60,000. On 13 September their performance at the Golders Green Hippodrome was taped for Radio One's respected 'In Concert' series and the programme went out the following month. Trident then set about planning the group's first national tour of theatres, as opposed to pubs and clubs, a Herculean task which attained fruition only when a great deal of money exchanged hands between the company and Bob Hirschmann, the manager of American rock-band Mott The Hoople, whom they eventually supported. Hirschmann had been unwilling to take on Queen, it emerged, because their first single, *Keep Yourself Alive*, had failed to chart in the United States and the money – at the time said to be for the financing of Queen's PA equipment and spectacular lighting – was in effect a thinly disguised insurance policy, just in case they failed to make the grade.

The try-outs for the tour took Queen to Europe. In Paris they appeared on France-Inter's long-running radio show, 'Pop-Club', hosted by José Artur. Then, after several gigs, radio and television programmes in Belgium and Holland, the group played their first open-air concert at the Frankfurt Bagodesburg. While in Germany Freddie paid a clandestine visit to one of the city's notorious leather bars which offered him a taste of the overt gay macho culture which, a few years later, he would triumphantly introduce to the stage. In London, besides a rip-roaring performance at the Paris Theatre, there were two gigs at Imperial College – the one of 2 November being Queen's first sell-out performance.

The tour kicked off at the Leeds Town Hall on 12 November, where Queen performed numbers from their début album, tested the water with tracks from their forthcoming one, and threw in a few standards such as *Big Spender*, the song from *Sweet Charity* which had been a big hit for Shirley Bassey and Peggy Lee. For this Freddie was at his most outrageous, strutting about the stage like a peacock and encouraging the audience to join him in the refrain. There were innumerable reviews in the music press, again mostly bad. As would years later happen with the Morrissey concerts of the Nineties, some of the hack journalists appeared to have witnessed an entirely different concert from the one the fans had seen, and liked to think that they were intelligently dissecting it when in reality they were mostly interested not in the music but in making offensive personal remarks about the artists. The quartet took it all in their stride, adopting the maxim, 'Better to be kicked than ignored.' And in any case, as the tour progressed through nineteen further venues, it became increasingly obvious that their fanbase was swelling at an incredible but welcome rate – and that audiences of all ages were more interested in seeing this exciting new band than the one topping the bill.

For the time being, however, Mott The Hoople were the bigger band, and when they told their management that maybe Queen should also support them on their 1974 American tour, there were no arguments.

On 3 December 1973, the day after their penultimate concert at Chatham Central, Queen taped their second session for the BBC's 'Sound of the Seventies' with Bernie Andrews. This time they chose *Great King Rat*, *Son and Daughter* and *Modern Times Rock 'N' Roll* from their first album, and *Ogre Battle* from its soon-to-be-released successor. The eight songs from the sessions remained in the BBC archives for another sixteen years, when they were put out on the album 'Queen at the Beeb'. Then, as in 1973, it was Freddie's *Ogre Battle* which was awarded the most accolades. 'A panorama of virulent grandeur and broadsword clashing mania', was how Malcolm Dome of *RAW* magazine reviewed it, while Paul Elliot of *Sounds* saw the whole concept as, 'Quaint, plush, pompous, ritzy-kitsch de-luxe metal . . . Spartacus in sequins!'

With 'Queen II' completed, at the end of January 1974 the group flew to Australia for two concerts at the Sunbury Music Festival, near Melbourne. The brief tour was a disaster. Brian was suffering the after-effects of a gangrenous infection in his arm, caused by a dirty needle used during the mandatory inoculations for the trip. Freddie had tinnitus and could not hear properly. At Sunbury there was a great deal of bitchiness in the promoters' camp on account of the hype which Queen awarded themselves – driving everywhere in a hired limo, while the other acts had to stick to battered old vans, and turning up for photo-shoots looking immaculate but very much out of place in silks and velvets when everyone else was wearing T-shirts and jeans. 'We're not trying to be different,' Freddie told one journalist. 'If you're a professional, darling, you don't have to *try* to be anything!' The worst came when Queen were introduced on stage by a famous chat-show host who, not content with leading the crowd in a slow-handclap, bared his buttocks, broke wind into the microphone, and pronounced, 'That's what *I* think of those stuck-up Pommie bastards!' those closest to the stage did actually enjoy Queen's set, brief as it was. Halfway through the lighting-rig exploded, plunging the stage into darkness, sabotaged by local electricians, angry with the group for having brought out their own crew instead of using the on-site workforce. Not surprisingly, Queen cancelled the following evening's show – the 'official' reason given was that Brian and Freddie were indisposed – and a few days later, at their own expense, they and their entourage returned to England. At Heathrow their plane was met by a bevvy of reporters and press photographers who had been misinformed that it was *the* Queen who was arriving! Freddie posed and pouted, but he and the rest of the group were ignored, barring one reporter who dismissed them as 'a bunch of long-haired layabouts'.

In February, in a decision which must have shocked the music press, the readers of *New Musical Express* voted Queen runners-up (after Leo Sayer) for Most Promising New Name – unusual considering they had had no chart success whatsoever, though this was remedied at the end of the month when EMI distributed promotional copies of *Seven Seas of Rhye*, c/w *See What a Fool I've Been*. The song had appeared on Queen's first album but this longer, updated version was from the forthcoming 'Queen II'.

The group were taken under the wing of Ronnie Fowler, the head of EMI's promotions department – who just happened to be one of Queen's biggest fans. For several days Fowler pestered radio and television producers, and his coup paid off when, on 21 February – as the result of the promotional film for David Bowie's 'Rebel, Rebel' failing to get to the studio on time – the group were offered a last-minute spot on 'Top of the Pops'. Therefore, in the days when the pop-show actually made the ratings, millions of viewers were treated to what the *Sunday Times* called, 'Led Zeppelin in frocks's contribution to glam rock . . . pure Freddie Mercury, massively entertaining, superbly artificial and enigmatic to the point of meaninglessness'.

Television audiences certainly had seen nothing quite like Queen since the days of the outrageous New York Dolls. With his almost androgynous porcelain features framed by a dense curtain of dark, silky hair and sporting an excruciatingly tight catsuit which revealed a generous expanse of hirsute torso, this particular frontman was ten

times more exciting – and talented – than any other of the
last two decades.

Henceforth, for Queen it would be roses all the way. Such
was the demand for the single that EMI were given just two
days to get it into the shops. Radio One played it to death,
and within a matter of weeks it had peaked at Number 10 in
the charts – and Queen were planning their first headlining
tour. As for the 'Led Zeppelin connection', John Deacon, the
least vociferous member of the group, angrily kicked this
into touch by telling the press, '*We're* more structured, and a
lot more intricate planning goes into *our* music, especially in
the recording studio!'

Queen's success resulted in Freddie giving up his stall on
Kensington Market, not that he had spent much time there of
late. Rehearsals for the tour took place at Ealing Studios,
with all the stops pulled out to ensure its success in a climate
which was financially unsound – Britain had been hit by the
three-day week and the oil crisis. 'Queen II' had been
scheduled for release before the twenty-two-date tour – this
began at Blackpool's Winter Garden Theatre on 1 March –
but because of a government restriction on electricity it did
not come out until eight days later. Dismissing it as 'the dregs
of glam rock', *Record Mirror* concluded, 'If *this* band are our
brightest hope for the future, we're committing rock and roll
suicide.' *Melody Maker*, speculating over Queen's proposed
tour of the United States, which one journalist prophesied
would either make or break them, responded smugly, 'If they
do, I'll eat my hat!'

The fans, of course, proved the press wrong each evening
by chanting 'God Save the Queen' before the group went on
stage, and by screaming for encores after they had left.
Hundreds of letters were sent to Trident and EMI, leading to
the creation of an official fan club, set up and run initially by
sisters Pat and Sue Johnstone, two of Roger's friends from
Truro. The fans were also rushing out to buy the new album,
which soared to Number 5 in the charts, while the

re-released 'Queen' peaked at Number 24. Both albums stayed in the charts for well over six months.

The tour had its share of incidents, some caused by fans, others aggravated by the group themselves. At Stirling University on 16 March, a brawl erupted in the auditorium after the concert, when an exhausted Queen did not make it into their fourth encore, and two fans were stabbed. Ten days later, at a post-gig party in their hotel on the Isle of Man, drunken revellers smashed up the room and Queen were told by island authorities, 'We never want to see you or your people here again.'

The tour should have ended on 31 March with the gig at the Rainbow Theatre, in London's Finsbury Park. However, because of the fracas in Stirling, the 17 March show at Barbarella's nightclub in Birmingham had been postponed – ostensibly to allow the rough element among the group's camp-followers to settle down – and it now took place on 2 April. Here, following a 'dare' from Roger Taylor, two members of Queen's road crew and the lead singer from the support band, Nutz, added mayhem to the proceedings by streaking several times across the stage.

Queen's first American tour, supporting Mott The Hoople, opened in Denver on 16 April, but the locals, unaccustomed to seeing their rock stars in Zandra Rhodes's silks, nail varnish and make-up, initially regarded them as a joke. Gradually, however, they gained momentum and press approval until 7 May, when they began a six-night stint on Broadway. The venue was the plush Uris Theater, famous for its Tennessee Williams' and Rachel Crothers' social dramas, but thus far in its history never host to a rock concert. All should have been well. The entire week was a sell-out, Queen were sensational, and the reviews mostly good. Unlike their British counterparts the American music press never mounted a smear campaign against the group. However, the fans made a nuisance of themselves, causing thousands of dollars' worth of damage by urinating in the auditorium, and completely ruining the beautiful old carpets by putting their cigarettes out on them. Thus, as with the Isle of Man, Queen were told not to darken the sidewalks of Broadway again.

Queen might have been able to cope with this drama – they did, after all, pay for damage which had been caused by someone else – had it not been for the sudden curtailment of the tour. Just as they were doing so well, Brian May collapsed with what was at first thought to be food poisoning. It was very much worse than that – hepatitis, the result of the same infected needle which had caused all the trouble on the eve of the trip to Australia.

The group returned to England in the middle of May, having promised to resume the American tour later in the year. Brian was taken to hospital, where he remained for four weeks, initially in a critical condition. There then followed a mad dash to get inoculated everyone who had been in contact with him during the last few months. Even so, Brian steadfastly refused to vegetate and from his sickbed worked on the new songs for Queen's next album, 'Sheer Heart Attack'.

Once Brian was back on his feet, the group began working in the studio. Then in August, when the album was almost complete, Brian was taken ill with a perforated ulcer and rushed to King's College Hospital, where surgeons carried out an emergency operation. He came out of hospital with enough time to spare to overdub those small sections of the album where, due to illness, his playing had not been up to scratch, before attending a reception at London's Café Royal on 5 September – Freddie's twenty-eighth birthday – where Queen were presented with their silver disc for selling 100,000-plus copies of 'Queen II'. The accolade was handed to them by Queen Elizabeth II lookalike Jeanette Charles, which caused Freddie to muse, 'You'd think she'd have gone all the way and invited us to Buckingham Palace!'

On 11 October, two of the numbers from 'Sheer Heart

Attack' were released on a double-A side – *Killer Queen* and *Flick of the Wrist*, both written by Freddie. The single recompensed all their hard work by peaking at Number 2 in the British charts and gave Queen their first Top Twenty hit in the United States. It was also a hit in several European countries. In France *Killer Queen* became that winter's gay anthem and at the famous Piano-Zinc club in Paris – an establishment where entry is free so long as one does a 'turn' – dozens of Freddie lookalikes took to the stage to perform it *a cappella*, stopping the show each night for several weeks. The journalist Alain Lavanne, confessing that it was his favourite Queen song, called it, 'A copulation of hard-on guitars and vaginal vocals which gives off a heady, forbidden perfume before exploding into a steamhammering orgasm!'

As there was now no question of them returning to the United States before early 1975, Queen emarked on an eighteen-date British tour which began at Manchester's Palace Theatre on 30 October. More often than not, each meticulously rehearsed show began 'continental-style' – the stage area plunged into total darkness, a brief overture, and Freddie's sudden materialization in a single spotlight to deliver the first few bars of *Now I'm Here* before the rest of the group joined in.

From then on their set would rapidly gather momentum – fireworks, dry ice and spectacular effects from the huge new lighting-rig. Julianne Regan, the pretty singer with the now disbanded All About Eve, saw Queen for the first time on 3 November at the Apollo Theatre, Coventry. She said of Freddie, 'I thought he was gorgeous, and loved the way he flicked his wrists when he played the piano. He was a jamboree bag of After Eight Mints, champagne, red roses, satin and silver – tastefully tacky and immensely talented, an absolute bundle of charisma and the unsurpassable king of weird and wonderful vocal harmonies.'

The fans were generally better behaved during this tour than the previous one, though there were problems in

Glasgow on 8 November. This was the day 'Sheer Heart Attack' was released, and several overzealous fans grabbed Freddie when he moved too close to the edge of the stage, pulling him head first into the pit. Luckily he was unhurt, though after the show ten rows of seats were completely destroyed. However, rather than present Queen with a bill for damages, the manager of the Apollo Theatre handed each member a silver statuette – for the first time ever, HOUSE FULL notices had been pasted on its hoardings.

The tour should have ended on 19 November with Queen's gig at the Rainbow – their only London concert – but such was the demand for tickets that the promoters tagged on an extra performance for the following evening. Both concerts were filmed – the thirty-minute *Queen at the Rainbow* was shown in provincial cinemas in 1976, supporting the Burt Reynolds film *Hustle*, while the complete version was only ever included in the mail-order-only 'Box of Tricks', issued in 1992 and way beyond the price-range of most fans. The tape-recording also remains elusive. Intended for use on a live album, it was archived because Trident believed that fans who had bought Queen's three albums would complain of being ripped off by buying the same songs again.

In fact, many people believed that Trident were the ones doing the ripping off. Though they travelled, lodged, ate, and even had fun in great style, Queen were still only getting £80 each per week from their management, who had recently bought their second Rolls-Royce! 'Theirs was an impossible situation,' said Barbara Baker, their producer's wife. 'Freddie wanted to buy a piano and John Deacon needed just two thousand pounds for the deposit on a little house because he was getting married. And Norman Sheffield would say, "Who do you think you *are*? We can't give you *money*!" ' For the time being, however, an uneasy truce was maintained.

Three days after the Rainbow, Queen flew to Sweden for a concert in Gothenburg, followed by dates in Finland,

Belgium, Germany, Holland and Spain. There were only ten shows – several others had to be cancelled when the PA truck was involved in an accident – but every one was a sell-out, the 6,500 tickets for Barcelona being snapped up in just eight hours, causing Freddie to fall in love with the city which some years later would almost become synonymous with his name.

Queen returned to the United States at the end of January 1975, two weeks after John Deacon's marriage to his long-time girlfriend, Veronica Tetzlaff – and while their second single from the album, *Now I'm Here*, c/w *Lily of the Valley*, had entered the British charts, where it would reach Number 11. This time, however, there was little doubting their success – all thirty concerts sold out well in advance and additional dates were tagged on as the tour progressed, sometimes involving two performances in the same day, and in early April Queen crossed the border for two concerts in Canada.

For Freddie, who had developed a throat infection ten days into the tour – a problem which would bug him for the rest of his life, on account of too much on-stage shouting and too many cigarettes – the whole experience was a triumph of mind over matter. There were times when his doctors forbade him to speak, let alone sing, advice he usually ignored, and Queen were fortunate that only a few dates had to be cancelled. The tour ended in Seattle on 6 April, after which the group flew to Hawaii – their first holiday together – to wind down in preparation for their first visit to Japan.

Freddie, who even this early in his career appeared to be developing an aversion for speaking about his personal life – perhaps because he was constantly trying to avoid the sneers of the British music press – had come very close to being 'outed' in Ohio, early in February. The American press (and for the time being their British counterpart) knew absolutely nothing about his discreet post-gig forays into the gay scene of each town or city on the tour circuit and that, unable to do so in Ohio, he had 'bought in' from an agency specializing in such things. Thus when he was interviewed by David Hancock of the fortunately obscure *Record Popswop Mirror*, he almost came unstuck when Hancock was shown into his hotel room thirty minutes early . . . to find Freddie reclining on a pile of cushions, being waited on hand and foot by three scantily clad muscular young hunks. The reporter – in his feature, he referred to Freddie as 'The Quicksilver Girl' – was curious to know why he was apparently incapable of fixing himself a drink or lighting his own cigarettes. Nothing was mentioned about the real reason the young men were there. Freddie told Hancock, expecting to be believed, 'They're *servants*, dear. I just love being pampered – it's just something that's grown with me. I mean, I can't even make myself a cup of tea. I'm useless at it, so I have someone else to do it for me. That's the kind of environment I live in, my dear!'

3

Pay the Bill . . .
Taste the Wine

When Queen arrived in Tokyo on 18 April 1975, both 'Sheer Heart Attack' and *Killer Queen* were in the lower reaches of the Japanese charts, and at the airport they were mobbed by over 3,000 fans – something which so far had not happened in Britain or the United States. 'Suddenly, we were the Beatles,' Brian reflected. 'We literally had to be carried over the heads of these kids . . . this wasn't a rock band thing, this was being a teen idol.'

The idolatry, in fact, had less to do with them being Queen than with the Japanese's love of great camp icons. The *tragédiennes* of French song have all – with the exception of Piaf, who refused to perform there because of the country's wartime atrocities – been immensely successful there. In 1975, twenty-five years after her last tour of Japan, the *réaliste* singer Damia was still getting into the charts with her

41

songs of suicide and despair. And Freddie, with his over-the-top dramatics – one Japanese newspaper described him as 'a cross between *kabuki* and *le cinéma muet*' – was like Bowie, Elton John, Marc Almond and the later Morrissey in every sense a drama-queen, something he admitted himself.

The first of Queen's eight concerts in Japan took place the following evening at the immense 10,000-seater Budokan, a stadium usually reserved for martial arts, where the management had dispensed with the usual type of security and had employed thirty sumo wrestlers to prevent fans from getting too close to the stage. They proved useless against the ensuing pandemonium when several hundred mostly teenage girls surged forward in a massive wave, flattening the flimsy seating and scrambling over the wrestlers. Then, the instant Freddie raised his hand, as if warding off a blow, they all retreated to what was left of their seats.

The tour progressed with equal hysteria through Nagoya, Kobe, Fukuoka – 'And the same to you, dear!', was Freddie's response, the first time he heard the name – Okayama, Shizuoka and Yokohama. Each member of the group had his personal bodyguard, and for their own safety they travelled between venues in armoured cars or vans. Everywhere they went they were showered with gifts – sometimes flowers, occasionally expensive items, such as the lovely kimonos they wore for their return to the Budokan on 1 May for their final concert . . . by which time their album and their single were topping the Japanese charts.

Freddie developed two passions while in Japan: art and geisha boys. Jackie Gunn, who now co-runs the Queen Fan Club, told me:

Anything Japanese, Fred would buy it. It started off with small things he could bring through customs without paying the duty. As he became richer, he brought more. Statuettes, paintings, screens, dolls. You name it, he bought it. One year he bought us all the most beautiful silk kimonos. He was always generous, always kind to his friends.

His second fascination was for the world of the Ginza, the most lively and colourful thoroughfare in Tokyo, long favoured by both tourists and artists, almost a Japanese Pigalle or Soho. During this and each subsequent stay in the city, he would make discreet visits to the notorious but classy *kagé-me-jaya* (tea-houses in the shadows), founded after the Second World War by American GIs, where for the appropriate fee customers were able to sample the delights of one or more of the geisha boys whose names appeared on the menu next to the food. He met Japan's most accomplished female impersonator, Miwa (Akihuro Maruyama), then aged forty-two and exquisitely beautiful. Known as the Japanese Piaf, Miwa directed his own cabaret on the Ginza, and in the late Seventies started adding Freddie Mercury songs to his extensive repertoire, as a tribute to his importance among the *kagé-me-jaya* fraternity.

According to Miwa, more than any other entertainer Freddie epitomized the archetypal *gai-jin*, as foreigners are called in Japan, because Western men are usually bigger, better-endowed and more hirsute than their Oriental counterparts. But if any of these geisha boys were hoping to add Freddie's name to their list of clientele, they would be sorely disappointed. According to his friends, the singer would have absolutely no amorous interest in what he called 'the little people'; he simply liked them to pamper him and wait on him hand and foot.

Returning to England, Queen coped with the growing burden of their management and financial problems by immediately getting to work on their next album. All four members of the group were deeply in debt to sound and lighting companies. John Deacon in particular was finding it hard making ends meet, still living in a bedsit, and with a

baby on the way. (His son, Robert, was born in July.) Yet
their popularity had done nothing but escalate during their
time abroad. The readers of one music magazine, *Disc*, had
voted them Best British, International and Live Group, and
Killer Queen Best Single. On 22 May Freddie received an
Ivor Novello Award for the same song, causing a rumpus
among the other nominees, who did not believe that
pop-songs warranted such accolades. In Belgium the song
won a prestigious Lion d'Or ... yet Trident's seemingly
feeble excuse for not being able to give the group a pay rise
was that it had cost the company too much money already –
just under £200,000, they claimed – sending them all over
the world. They were therefore left with no alternative than
to place the matter in the hands of their lawyer, Jim Beach.

Freddie's lover at this time was David Minns, a
dark-haired, well-built man who had worked for Paul and
Linda McCartney for a while before turning his talents
towards music publishing. Minns had just taken a young
singer-songwriter under his wing: Eddie Howell had already
released three singles and a promising début album, 'The
Eddie Howell Gramophone Record'. Now, in between
composing material for Queen's new album, Freddie began
showing an avid interest in Howell's career. Having listened
to the demo of *The Man From Manhattan*, a song about the
Mafia, Freddie announced that he would like to produce it.

Howell was invited to the Holland Road flat, where Freddie
went through the song just once on his grand piano before
deciding that he would also sing the backing vocals. Not only
this, Brian May was persuaded to provide lead guitar, and
Mike Stone – Queen's recording engineer – was brought in as
well! The recording sessions took place at the Sarm Studios,
but dragged on for almost a week on account of Freddie's
meticulous attention to detail – in one instance, a single note D
which ended the song, when any number of substitutes would
have sufficed. Not to be thwarted, Freddie spent £800 of his
own money on a motorcycle courier who scoured London's

music shops until a suitable bell could be found. He then told his friend, 'If this isn't a hit, dear, you should sue Warner Brothers!' Though successful in parts of Europe, the record proved a costly flop in Britain – not because it was mediocre but because Eddie Howell's bass player was not British and a Member of the Musicians Union, and therefore the record was banned from the airwaves.

At the end of August Queen were able to break free of their contract with Trident – but at a staggering cost. In order to record directly for EMI, they were compelled to sign a severance contract with Trident, the terms of which were an immediate down-payment of £100,000 – which they did not even have a fraction of – and one per cent of the royalties from their next six albums. Freddie told the *New Musical Express*, 'As far as Queen are concerned, our old management is deceased. They cease to exist in any capacity with us whatsoever. One leaves them behind like one leaves excreta. We feel so relieved!' Trident reciprocated by dumping the group's PA equipment in an alley outside the studio – in the rain.

Queen also dispensed with the services of their publicist, Tony Brainsby, and aided by Jim Beach – now a close friend – they began an urgent search for a new manager. After several setbacks, they settled on John Reid, then managing Elton John. His advice was very sound: the group should leave their problems to the experts – his lawyers – and get on with what they were good at: making records.

John Reid and Jim Beach entered into negotiations with EMI and quickly persuaded them to advance Queen the money to pay off their 'debt' to Trident, though their troubles with the company would continue for a little longer. The deal was clinched with a lavish party on 19 September at the London Coliseum, where the group were presented with a selection of gold and silver discs for all three of their albums, as well as for *Killer Queen*.

Queen's new album was given the title 'A Night at the

Opera', after the classic Marx Brothers' comedy film, and its pre-publicity proclaimed it one of the most expensive albums ever made – at an estimated cost of £35,000. It took three months to record, in six different studios, and with a great deal of the in-production tension and tantrums which perfectionism invariably creates.

Unquestionably, the album's *pièce de résistance* was Freddie's *Bohemian Rhapsody*, a pioneering rock *symphonie en miniature*, almost six minutes long, which took three weeks to record, and which Freddie insisted would be Queen's next single. Their management was wholly against the idea. It was twice the length of an average single, they declared, and would never get any air-play. Freddie recalled in *Rockline*, some years later, 'They wanted to chop it down to three minutes. I said, "It either stays as it is, or forget it!" It was either going to be a big flop or a big hit. A risk element is always involved and that's the way I like it. That's what makes good music!'

The single was released on 31 October, backed with Roger Taylor's *I'm In Love With My Car* and attractively packaged in Queen's first-ever British picture sleeve – and the rest is, to borrow an old cliché, history. On 7 November, seven days before the group's new British tour, it and the album were premièred for the largely indifferent media at London's Roundhouse Studios. Freddie's pal Kenny Everett played it fourteen times during two consecutive weekend shows on London's Capital Radio, and it shot straight up the charts, holding the Number One slot for nine weeks – beating the record set in 1957 by Paul Anka's *Diana*.

Everett remembered the first time he heard the song:

Freddie plonked it on the machine, and this glorious operatic wonder came out. I remember him being unsure about this pile of genius – it was like Mozart saying he didn't know if his clarinet concerto was going to take off. *Bohemian Rhapsody* had Number One written all over it from the first note.

The song won Queen their first platinum disc, a British Phonographic Industry Award for Best Single of 1975, a second Ivor Novello Award for Freddie and, if this were not enough, at the 1977 Brit Awards it was named joint Best Pop Single of the Last Twenty-Five years with Procul Harum's *A Whiter Shade of Pale*.

Bohemian Rhapsody also set another invaluable precedent, a trend without which today's pop industry would be virtually useless – the promotional video. Promotional films, of course, were nothing new in the music business. Badly edited fragments of monochrome film survive from the American jazz age, hopelessly out of synch, and the French star Marie Dubas had used a film-clip in 1936 to promote her million-selling *Mon Légionnaire*, a song which Freddie adored in the later version by Edith Piaf. Today, the videos are sadly more often than not much more interesting than the songs they are promoting – Adam and the Ants's *Prince Charming*, for example, loses much of its magic when heard and not seen. But Queen's video for *Bohemian Rhapsody* was the very first time a pop song had used the medium. Freddie's contribution to it was pure Grand Guignol – hunching his slender frame over the grand piano in a parody of Paderewski, crossing his hands while raising them from the keys to an absurd level with his chin. The original plan was that the video should be used as a stand-in should Queen be too busy touring to appear on 'Top of the Pops'. It was directed by Bruce Gower, the man responsible for *Queen at the Rainbow*, and was filmed at Elstree in four hours, for just £4,500, a mere drop in the ocean compared with some less presentable modern 'epics', but it was a major contributory factor towards the song's staggering success around the world. 'Try making *that* on your Super-8 at home!' enthused DJ Dave Lee Travis, after it had received its television première, and in its entirety. The video also offered Queen something they had never had before – a silhouette, in this instance a conjoined, quadruple head-and-shoulders shot of them gazing up into a spotlight, which became almost as synonymous with their image as Freddie's crest.

The great mystery surrounding *Bo Rap*, as it is affectionately known by fans, is that no one really knew what it was about. Moreover, its composer was reticent when speaking about it, saying, 'I want people to listen to it, think about it, then decide for themselves what it means to them.'

The music press, of course, could not leave it there and, fourteen years after its release they would still be pulling it to pieces. The *New Musical Express*, borrowing a line from the song, devised a regular feature entitled 'BISMILLAH . . . NO! We Will Not Let Him Go: The World's Worst Lyrics', in which musically challenged 'experts' – Freddie called them 'wankers' – panned such standards as Bobby Goldsboro's *Honey*, Band Aid's *Feed the World* and even Elvis Presley's *Jailhouse Rock*.

The opening song on 'A Night at the Opera', *Death on Two Legs*, caused Queen untold problems with their former management, for when Trident executive Norman Sheffield saw the bracketed subtitle, 'Dedicated to . . .', and listened to lines such as 'You suck my blood like a leech/You've taken all my money and you want more!', he knew only too well that they were directed at him. Worse still were the 'sewer-rat' and 'barrow-boy' references and the damning, 'But now you can kiss my ass goodbye!' Needless to say, there was soon talk of an injunction preventing the album's release – or, at least, the removal of this song.

The group stood their ground. Although the lyrics were autobiographical, no lawyer would have been able to prove that they were an attack against Trident, though EMI are alleged to have paid the company a large sum of hush money to persuade them to drop their action, which they did. Gary Langan, a record producer who worked with Queen on 'Sheer Heart Attack' and their next three albums, remembered the actual recording session and recalled how

Freddie had worked himself up into such a fury that blood had come out of his ears. He added, 'No one would ever believe how much hate and venom went into both the singing of that song, let alone the lyrics themselves.'

Queen's now annual tour opened at the Liverpool Empire on 14 November 1975. This time the costumes would be more outrageous than ever before and different for almost every show, the lighting more spectacular and costly, the music louder and more evocative. Some nights Freddie wore one of the kimonos he had brought back from Japan, or just multicoloured tights which left absolutely nothing to the imagination – and left many people wondering if he really was gay, or was just having everyone on. It was at around this time, too, that he began doing exciting things with his detachable microphone stand, turning it into an essential prop. It would ably serve as barbell, guitar, golf-club, hatchet, baton, neck-exerciser . . . and penis extension!

Acknowledging that Queen were now the biggest band in Britain, James Johnson of the *London Evening Standard* interviewed Freddie in Birmingham on 10 December and asked him, quite bluntly, if his 'camp demeanour' was really a part of his personality. The singer's response was equally to the point, and not a 'dear' in sight. 'Are you asking whether I'm bisexual? If I told you, it would destroy all the mystery. I move in a theatrical world and people can draw their own connotations from that. I have a girlfriend I have lived with for five years. I have boyfriends as well.' There was also another thinly veiled reference to Queen's tribulations with Trident when he added, 'You have to be prepared to build up a defence if you're really into it for the big time, otherwise you get eaten up. I always say that success *has* changed me because it has made me vicious . . . the whole *group* have become more vicious, more calculating.'

Freddie's almost ruthless perfectionism was a constant theme running throughout David Evans's 1992 biography,

This is the Real Life, co-written with David Minns, and drawing on innumerable reminiscences from friends, admirers and colleagues. Evans, who had worked for John Reid Enterprises in the capacity of general manager, wrote, 'He was the sort of man you're thrilled to have as a friend, but desperately relieved not to have to wake up next to on a bad morning.' The Metropolis Studios' Gary Langan, who worked with Queen on four of their albums, recalled in the same publication that, on account of his moods, Freddie was quite frightening as a person. He concluded, 'He wasn't very approachable. If you were going to be his friend, you knew it was going to be something you had to work on . . . a friendship with Freddie was not something that he was going to accept at a glance.'

Meanwhile, each venue on the 1975 tour-circuit was a complete sell-out, and there was little trouble with fans. There was one incident after their concert in Newcastle on 11 December when, according to the local police, 'an interested party' tipped them off that the group were carrying drugs. Their coach was stopped outside Dundee, where they were escorted to the nearest station to be searched. The police must have been truly disappointed to have found only a small bottle of headache pills.

On 29 November Queen had begun a four-night stint at London's Hammersmith Odeon which had proved such a success that they were asked to return there on Christmas Eve, the day after their tour should have ended, for a show which was broadcast live both on BBC2's 'The Old Grey Whistle Test' and Radio One. The event was doubly important for Freddie and Brian May, whose parents were in attendance. Like their sons, they had been virtual neighbours for years and were now meeting for the first time. Exactly what Bomi and Jer Bulsara thought of their son, camping it up to the nines in front of thousands of ecstatic fans is anybody's guess, not to mention all the mincing, effing and blinding which occurred during the post-gig party. They did, however, put on a tremendous show of good manners and correct etiquette which impressed everyone, and shared in their son's delight when 'A Night at the Opera', released on 21 November, reached Number One soon afterwards.

Queen's long-overdue American tour began on 27 January 1976 at the Palace Theater in Waterbury, Connecticut, where audiences were confused by their opening number, *Now I'm Here*. The lines were alternated by Freddie and the group's personal assistant Pete Brown miming to his voice, the pair standing at opposite ends of the stage and wearing identical costumes. As with their previous visit to the United States, it took over a week for the tour to build up momentum. Freddie refused to socialize with company executives and record promoters, attending only the post-gig parties he had organized, and neither *Bohemian Rhapsody* nor 'A Night at the Opera' were getting sufficient air-play, though this had been rectified by 5 February, when Queen played the first of four gigs at New York's Beacon Theater. The single reached Number 9 in the charts and the album Number 4. Also while in New York they bumped into Ian Hunter of Mott the Hoople, who persuaded them to harmonize on *You Nearly Done Me In*, one of the tracks from his forthcoming solo album. And towards the end of the thirty-three-date tour, they received the welcoming news that all four of their albums were currently in the British charts.

After America, Queen flew to Japan for eleven concerts. They had learned several phrases phonetically in Japanese, and very nearly caused a riot at the Budokan the first time Freddie pronounced one of them. From Japan they flew to Australia, for a part of their contract which they had been reluctant to fulfil. This time, however, there was only enthusiasm. The vulgar television presenter was nowhere to be seen, each of their eight concerts had been sold out for weeks, and both their album and their single were topping the charts. They returned to England to begin working on their next album towards the end of April 1976, and on 29 May Brian May married his sweetheart, Chrissy Mullen, at the Roman Catholic Church in Barnes.

At around this time British newspapers began speculating over cracks which they said had begun appearing in Freddie's relationship with Mary Austin – according to the tabloids, because he had recently confessed his bisexuality to her. This, and further newspaper allegations that Mary was beginning to find Freddie an embarrassment, could only, of course, have been pure fabrication. During the summer of 1976 Freddie's antics were no more over-the-top than they had been years before when Mary had first met him – and even after their meticulously planned parting the pair still saw as much of each other as Queen's hectic touring and recording schedule permitted.

Freddie owed this woman so much, and henceforth his generosity towards her would be boundless and, as much as was possible, kept from the media. He and Mary had decided upon having their own space while Queen had been touring. 'I'd been living in the same little Kensington flat for ages,' he told James Johnson of the *Evening Standard*. 'So I phoned Mary, my girlfriend, from America and asked her to find us a place.'

Freddie had recently relocated to another flat in Stafford Terrace, but when Mary sent him photographs of Garden Lodge, a huge Georgian mansion in Kensington's Logan Place, set in a quarter-acre of semi-landscaped garden, yet all tucked clandestinely away behind a ten-foot wall, he at once authorized her to purchase it, using £500,000 in cash. At the same time Freddie bought a luxury apartment for Mary, and for the umpteenth time tried to persuade his parents to let him buy them a more substantial property than the modest Feltham semi they had occupied since 1964. Stubbornly they refused his generosity yet again, hardly knowing how much this hurt his feelings. Rusi Dalal, a Parsee spokesman and friend of the Bulsaras, later explained their predicament:

'Freddie's parents were unhappy about his homosexuality. Being gay is not accepted in our religion, which as we have so very few believers can only be passed on from a father to his children. And as gay men do not normally have children – well, there lies the problem.'

Garden Lodge had been built as a vastly extended artist's studio for the Hoares, a wealthy family of merchant bankers, and Freddie of course could never resist referring to his new home as 'The Hoare House', though he did surprise friends by announcing that, for the time being at least, he would not be moving in, saying, 'Why should I, when I have a nice, comfortable flat?'

Freddie did begin an extremely costly four-year restoration programme on Garden Lodge, transforming a characterless, musty old house into a warm, breathing palatial residence, with eight bedrooms, four bathrooms, a multi-mirrored dressing-room, and even a minstrels' gallery – causing it to be dubbed 'The Graceland of Glam Rock' by one visiting reporter. Three rooms on the upper floor were knocked into one to form Freddie's bedroom, and he added a domed, illuminated roof which created any number of special 'mood' effects. His emperor bed was so heavy that it had to be hoisted up to the room by crane, and the electronic gadgets for this room alone are said to have cost in excess of £30,000.

Garden Lodge may have been Freddie's intended topic of conversation during his interview with the *Evening Standard*, which was conducted on the eve of Queen's free concert in Hyde Park. Sadly, this was a time when most journalists were only really interested in the 'Is-He-Or-Isn't-He?' aspect of his persona, particularly when he turned up, as then, clad in a white satin ensemble which was so tight around the middle that he had to unbutton the top of his trousers to sit down, with matching lurex socks, and with the fingernails of one hand painted black. Even so, while overcamping every anecdote and gesture, like Marc Bolan and Johnny Thunders he was able to pass himself off successfully as a heterosexual trapped within a hugely extroverted glam rock exterior.

An example of Freddie's fooling of the media occurred when James Johnson asked him if he and Mary would ever get around to 'tying the knot'. There was no hint that such a union would not take place, but an almost aspiring, 'Though we are very close, I don't really see us getting married for a while. Marriage is the kind of responsibility I don't want at this stage of my career.' All of which enabled Johnson to draw the conclusion which Freddie had manipulated: 'The whirlwind of success that Queen's exotic singer has become caught up in is such that there is no longer time for the niceties of life, like house-hunting or getting married.'

Some years later, when their split had long been public knowledge, Mary told the press, 'The more I knew Freddie, the more I grew to love him. You don't need a piece of paper to be married. *Our* marriage was in the heart. I've never felt that way about anybody, before or since.' After his death, however, she would be a little more forthcoming, telling his friend David Wigg that she would have felt jealous had Freddie been having other heterosexual relationships, but that she could never feel so about something she could never understand. 'I realized that I couldn't have him physically any more,' she would explain, 'but I could go on loving him mentally. I was strong enough to accept that he was bisexual or gay, and it never stopped me loving him. I never saw his boyfriends as a threat.'

Now, Freddie joked about how Mary had complained at his having an upright piano next to the bed – so that he could compose in the middle of the night, if need be – adding more seriously:

All my lovers have asked me why they couldn't replace Mary. She's the only true friend I have, and I don't *want* anybody else. To me, *she* was my common-law wife. To me, it *was* marriage. I couldn't fall in love with a man the way I did with Mary, and I'll love her until I draw my last breath.

During the first two days of September 1976 Queen participated in the Scottish Festival of Popular Music by giving two concerts at the recently refurbished Edinburgh Playhouse. Ten days later, they played an open-air show at Cardiff Castle in near-torrential rain without a single fan leaving the venue, and on 18 September – the sixth anniversary of Jimi Hendrix's death – their legendary free concert took place in London's Hyde Park.

The concert was billed as Queen's way of expressing their gratitude towards their British fans for supporting them over the past few years. By and large it had been orchestrated by Richard Branson, the founder of Virgin Records, not an easy task, for the conditions laid down by the Park authorities were stringent: exact start and finish times, with no running over, no alcohol whatsoever and the strictest security. Even the group were not allowed to arrive at the venue in their own cars. In full stage-gear they were smuggled through the gates in the back of a laundry van for what would be Hyde Park's biggest pop event since the Rolling Stones' eulogy to their drowned drummer, Brian Jones, seven years previously.

Not everyone, however, was confident of Queen's success. Harry Doherty, a journalist who had described their Edinburgh concerts as the best he had ever attended, told French rock magazine *More*, 'In spite of their obvious talent, I'm not at all convinced they will pull this thing off. It's too big, for one thing. Secondly, Queen are not yet important enough. They'll end up a laughing stock!' Doherty was proved wrong by an estimated 200,000 fans, considerably more than had turned up for the Stones, who flocked to the venue to persevere with support acts Supercharge, Steve Hillage and Kiki Dee – 'It would be *too* complimentary of me to describe *any* of them as better than mediocre,' observed

Doherty – before cheering Freddie as he strutted on to the stage to the strains of *Procession* in a white leotard. 'Welcome to our picnic by the Serpentine!' he piped, before launching into *Keep Yourself Alive*. Later in the show he wore a black leotard complete with diamanté codpiece – but there would be no encore, in spite of the massive roar of approval which went up after each song, particularly the newly composed *Tie Your Mother Down*, and Freddie's plaintive *You Take My Breath Away*, which he sang alone, accompanying himself on the piano. The concert was being broadcast live, by Kenny Everett, on Capital Radio, and filmed for inclusion in a Queen documentary to be transmitted later by the BBC, so the police were taking no chances. Freddie had been instructed that, should he so much as step on to the stage after the group's allotted 100-minute slot, he personally would be held responsible and arrested. In fact, this would not have been possible as, on the dot, the power was switched off, and even the crowd had to make their way out of Hyde Park in almost total darkness.

4

A Whisper on a
Star Chase

For Queen, one triumph followed another: two hit singles in Britain and the United States (*You're My Best Friend* and the gospel-like *Somebody to Love*), and an album which reached Number One in Britain and Number 5 in America. 'A Day at the Races', so named after another Marx Brothers' comedy film, was released with a fanfare of publicity on 10 December 1976. The press launch took place six days later at Kempton Park, when one of the races on the card was sponsored in its honour and won by John Francome on Lanzarote. And still the group were slated by the music press. 'Too formulated, too smartass, too reliant on trickery as a substitute for inspiration,' opined *Sounds*.

On 1 December, Queen inadvertently helped to create a slice of television history when work commitments forced them into the eleventh-hour cancellation of an appearance on Bill Grundy's chat show, 'Today'. EMI were asked to supply an alternative, and chose their latest punk acquisition, the Sex Pistols, without any doubt the most hyped, controversial and arguably talentless act of their day. In what must have been the most humiliating moment of his career, Grundy sat through the interview unable to stop the tirade of filthy language and atrocious behaviour which brought so many complaints from viewers that the Sex Pistols were dropped by EMI, and Grundy, the innocent bystander, was given the sack.

At the end of the year, the Queen Fan Club issued its very first 'biography' of the group. It was little more than a pamphlet but contained some excellent photographs, four stunning portraits of the individual members of the group, a list of all their awards and appearances to date, and individual questionnaires. Thus fans were able to learn that Brian May liked Natalie Wood but loathed Johnny Mathis, that John Deacon's favourite magazine was *Men Only*, and that Roger Taylor hated '98 per cent of music recorded today'. Some of Freddie's responses, of course, were typically outrageous:

* Hair/Eyes: Midnight black/liquid brown.
* Favourite Movies: Anything with Mae West.
* Favourite Food: Nectar.
* Favourite Drink: Champagne in a glass slipper.
* What were you doing before you started playing professionally?: A Kensington poseur.
* Your dream?: To remain the divine, lush creature that I am.
* Special talent other than music: Poncing and poovery.

On 13 January 1977, in sub-zero temperatures, Queen began a 40-plus-date tour of the United States at the Milwaukee Auditorium, initially supported by now-forgotten bands Head East and Cheap Trick, then by the Irish group Thin

Lizzy. In an attempt to capitalize on the Queen's Silver Jubilee later that summer, the promoters billed it 'The Queen Lizzy Tour'!

In America *Bohemian Rhapsody* was performed in its entirety for the first time – the multi-dubbed, 180-strong vocal section being replaced by a backing tape and a fireworks display while the group took a curtain-call. During the early days of the tour, however, the group were subjected to a vicious smear campaign from the American music press, who momentarily were almost as deliberately oblivious to Queen's talents as their British counterpart. Everything they performed, said and did, their appearance and personal lives, was denounced in the most vitriolic manner, whereas Thin Lizzy were praised beyond belief even by critics who had failed to attend their concerts. The ruse backfired, however, when many thousands of rock enthusiasts who were fans of neither group began flocking to venues out of sheer curiosity – only to come away as confirmed Queen addicts.

While in Los Angeles for two shows at the Forum on 3 and 4 March, Queen received a summons from Groucho Marx, inviting them to tea at his Hollywood home. The press temporarily shelved their attacks. If Groucho could rave about this bunch of English extroverts, then so could they for the moment so as not to offend one of their national institutions. They flocked to Beverley Hills to witness this most extraordinary scene. The elderly comic, in the last year of his life, had already sent the group a telegram congratulating them on the success of 'A Night at the Opera', and he was now photographed wearing the 'Queen II' tour jacket they had given him, along with an honorary engraved gold disc. There was also an impromptu recital when Groucho crooned a couple of his old film hits, and Queen sang Brian May's *39, a cappella*, in his living-room.

Back in England, however, Queen were still being persecuted by the music press, though this time there was slight consolation in the fact that they were not alone. Led

Zeppelin, Genesis and The Who were declared 'has-beens' in the wake of the horrendous punk explosion, and when Queen's otherwise excellent single *Tie Your Mother Down* only reached Number 31 in the charts, the death-knell was duly sounded. The fact that Queen stood for everything that this sudden cacophony of vulgarity did not: melody, comprehensible lyrics, taste, manners and sensibility, did not count for much with many rock journalists. Nor did Freddie's habit of toasting audiences with champagne and quips like 'People want art. They want showbiz. They *want* to see you rush off in your limousine!'

This latter statement formed the basis for Freddie's interview with Tony Stewart of the *New Musical Express*, a meeting which was peppered with expletives and bitchy asides reminiscent of those infamous Hedda Hopper–Louella Parsons feuds of the Thirties and Forties. The meeting was arranged by Freddie's new personal manager Paul Prenter, a twenty-six-year-old Irishman who had been brought in by John Reid and who, though a good friend at the time, would cause Freddie a great deal of grief in the future.

Exactly why Freddie agreed to such an interview is not known, bearing in mind that neither man could stand the sight of the other. It may well be that his sole intention was to avenge himself and Queen for the spite inflicted upon them by the music press over the last few years, and in particular this journalist who had already dismissed Freddie as 'A rock 'n' role spiv who uses his band as a vehicle for an elaborate exhibition of narcissism'. If so, it almost worked. Freddie did his utmost to make Stewart feel ill at ease, insisting that his burly bodyguard be present throughout the interview, and intimidating him at every opportunity. 'Seemingly he is determined that I should feel subordinate to him,' Stewart observed.

The bitching began within minutes, when Freddie told his antagonist, 'Darling, if everything you read in the press about me was true, I wouldn't be sitting here talking to you today. I'd be too worried about my ego!' Then, adding that he was living his life to the full he cracked, 'I hope that when *you* better yourself in your position you'll enjoy yourself, too!' When Stewart criticized Queen for their stagewear and glitzy performances, Freddie hit back with a tarty, 'What do *you* know about show business? Can you imagine doing the sort of things we've written, like *Rhapsody* and *Somebody To Love* in jeans, with absolutely no presentation?'

Stewart certainly gave the impression that he knew little about culture when, discussing Freddie's proposed tribute to the great Russian ballet dancer Vaslav Nijinsky, he suggested that most rock fans like himself would probably think Nijinsky was a famous racehorse, adding that in any case he was not qualified to review ballet. Freddie hit out with a sarcastic, 'What makes you think you're qualified to do rock 'n' roll?' The real venom surfaced, however, when inevitable comparisons were made between the British and American music press. 'The Americans don't have the same kind of prejudices,' Freddie observed scathingly. 'If they can do it, why the fuck can't people over here? You're too narrow minded. You're the bloody arrogant sods that just don't want to learn. You don't want to be told *anything*. You feel you know it all before it's even happened!'

His was a valid point. The publication had its revenge, however, by heading the subsequent feature, 'Is This Man a Prat?', and by insulting Freddie's intelligence by adding asides which he deemed 'pig-ignorant', such as, 'If I ever see Margot Fonteyn down the Rainbow, I'll buy her a pint!' He was further incensed by Stewart's gratuitous and quite unnecessary comment, 'His [Freddie's] fingers were vigorously pruning his hair, as if in search of nits.' Worse still was the acid observation, 'In this iconoclastic atmosphere there is nothing more redundant, or meaningless, than a posturing ballerina toasting the audience, as Mercury does, with, "May you all have champagne for breakfast!" ' Freddie flew into a rage, and swore that he would never speak to the music press again.

Queen returned home towards the end of March, though there was little time for resting up before leaving for Stockholm, early in May, to begin a brief European tour. Here, Freddie wore his famous 'L'Après-Midi d'un Faune' costume for the first time. The idea had been devised by Nijinsky himself for the Ballets Russes in 1912, and Freddie copied it lovingly down to the last detail, raising more than a few eyebrows among the clutch of reporters gathered backstage at the Ice Stadium who, for obvious reasons, could not avert their gaze from his crotch, by quipping, 'It's all me, darlings. I don't have my socks down there, or any coke bottle!' He then leapt on to the stage, executed a few pirouettes, and the audience went wild! Writing his review of the show, one of these journalists drew a comparison between Freddie and his current alter-image by applying to Freddie, the star, what Jean Cocteau had written about Nijinsky, the man:

> On one side of the curtain he was a marvel of grace, on the other an extraordinary example of strength and weakness . . .

Queen lost count of the accolades they received during this European tour, which culminated in a superb concert at the Basle sporthalle on 19 May. Two evenings previously at a boat party following their show at the Ahoy Hall in Rotterdam the group had been presented with an astonishing 35 silver, gold and platinum disks for record sales in Holland alone.

Flamboyance was the order of the day when Queen arrived back in Britain for a tour which concluded with two shows at London's Earls Court on 6 and 7 June. A banner, emblazoned with the announcement QUEEN IN CONCERT, was hung from the front of the building and at once sparked off the silliest of rows between the Mayor of Hammersmith and John Reid. The Mayor, upon seeing the banner, truly believed that *the* Queen had been booked to make a personal appearance as part of the borough's Jubilee celebrations, and that someone had forgotten to tell him! What happened next, however, was even more ridiculous, for someone from the Mayor's office actually contacted Buckingham Palace and demanded an explanation. Then, having learned the truth, the Mayor made an even bigger fool of himself by telephoning John Reid and demanding that the sign be taken down because it might confuse the public. It was in fact Freddie who responded on Reid's behalf, saying, 'Tell him I'll take it down myself, dear, and throttle the silly little man with it!'

At Earls Court Queen proudly revealed their new 'baby' – a 5,000-lb lighting-rig, shaped like a crown and measuring 54 × 26 feet, which rose slowly from the stage, exposing the group in a dazzling extravaganza of flashing beams. Over the next few years there would be several such crowns custom built for travelling, but this first one was the best and the most expensive – setting the group back a cool £50,000. And at the end of each concert, thousands of red, white and blue balloons were released into the audience to commemorate the Queen's Silver Jubilee. The music press attacked Queen for their 'pointless extravagance' and even had a dig at their music, mindless of the fact that the 36,000 tickets had sold in record time. What they did not mention was that the group had donated the proceeds from their second show plus the collection from a post-gig party held in a marquee in Holland Park – an alleged £100,000 – to the Jubilee Fund.

Queen's reverence and patriotism were a far cry from the disgraceful behaviour of their rivals, the Sex Pistols – for while there were mass pageantry and street-parties throughout Britain and the Commonwealth, their highly offensive *God Save The Queen* burst into the Top Ten and their manager, Malcolm McLaren, hosted a boat-party on the Thames which was attended by hundreds of fans sporting T-shirts depicting their sovereign wearing a safety-pin through her nose. A few weeks later, while Queen were working on their new album and the Sex Pistols were in an adjacent studio recording their 'Never Mind the Bollocks' album, Freddie bumped into their frontman, Sid Vicious, a thoroughly unpleasant, virulently homophobic individual who could not stand him. Freddie had the last word, however, when Vicious – referring to the Nijinsky costume – pronounced sarcastically, 'So, you've really brought ballet to the masses, then!' Quick as a flash, Freddie replied, 'Ah, Mr Ferocious. Well, we're trying our best, dear!'

Extravagance was the order of the day on 5 September 1977 when Freddie celebrated his thirty-first birthday at Cherry Brown's 'hip' Country Cousin restaurant on London's fashionable King's Road. The sumptuous bash was organized by his lover David Minns, who later confessed that the most expensive items on the bill were not the food and drink, but the thousands of flowers which decorated the establishment from top to bottom. Freddie had insisted on orchids even for the lavatories.

Each of the 150 invitations was handwritten by Freddie and bore the instruction 'Dress to kill!' The guest list, a veritable Who's Who of the famous and infamous, also included just about every record company big-wig in England, some of whom were used to outrageous and sometimes despicable behaviour from their clients. Even so, the slapstick antics of Elton John and Freddie's pal Kenny Everett were tame compared with those of the American diva, Divine, another great star who died far too young. Freddie had and would follow Divine's film and disco career with great enthusiasm, and told a French reporter after his friend had been awarded the nickname, 'The Filthiest Person Alive', 'Anyone who can eat *real* dog shit, dear, simply *has* to be a legend!' Now, the 340-pound, mini-skirted actor put on a show of his own. Ordering the nearly naked snake-charmer hired by Minns as part of the evening's entertainment to lie on top of a table, legs akimbo, he barked, 'And now, honey, for the orgasm of a lifetime!' before 'ejaculating' the entire contents of a magnum of champagne across her body. Freddie thanked him with a chirpy, 'Thanks, Divi. I'm so glad you could *come!*'

The hilarity aside, however, Freddie's relationship with Minns was falling apart at the seams, and would only deteriorate further the higher his particular star ascended. Like Mary Austin and several others, Minns could not accept taking a backseat while his lover was sleeping around indiscriminately. 'I couldn't hate him,' he said in the book he co-authored with David Evans. 'Yet neither did I kid myself that we would ever be best friends again. Our close friendship was a closed chapter.'

According to Paul Prenter, the relationship ended soon afterwards during a trip to Miami, when Freddie began making eyes at a hunky young American dancer named Dane Clark, who had once worked as Elton John's assistant and dresser. 'Minns screamed at Freddie, calling him a "faceless hussy",' Prenter recalled, explaining how in the hotel lift Minns had begun bashing Freddie over the head with a shoe, only to be smacked in the teeth. The singer, apparently undaunted, had then gone off to the beach with his latest 'catch', whom he had subsequently hired as his dresser, a position Clark retained until 1982.

Other friends, too, have spoken of how they were compelled to keep a more suitable distance as the potentially lethal combination of artistic temperament and fame began taking its toll, fuelled by those faithful allies of the *monstre sacré*: sex, drink, drugs and an acute neurasthenia brought on by the seemingly unsuccessful, interminable search for Mr Perfect.

Freddie's behaviour caused problems for the group, though not for John Reid as has been suggested. David Evans said, 'Queen and John Reid got together precisely because Freddie *was* gay. They were two gay men, working very well together. The three boys, however, always felt uncomfortable with Freddie's gayness. They weren't *scared* of it, just apprehensive. They didn't know how to handle it.'

Following the relative failure of their last single, Queen had released their first EP, 'Good Old Fashioned Lover Boy', which had only reached Number 17 in the charts, while Roger's début single, *I Wanna Testify*, had bombed completely. Brian's venture with Lonnie Donegan – playing on two tracks of the skiffle star's comeback album, 'Putting on the Style' – had fared slightly better, though these solo projects only pushed the tabloids into fabricating rumours that the group were about to split because they were incapable of coping with the competition from punk.

Queen's 'problem' was effectively solved by the October release of Freddie's stomping *We Are the Champions*, c/w Brian's equally anthemic *We Will Rock You*, a song which was considered just as important as the A-side, resulting in both numbers being given equal air-play in Britain, where the record reached Number 2 in the charts, and in the United States, where it peaked at Number 4, Queen's biggest hit there so far. *We Will Rock You* became the anthem of the New York Yankees, whereas *We Are the Champions* remains possibly the most played of all Queen's songs, and is regularly chanted on the terraces by football supporters worldwide, besides being included in television fitness and strength contests such as 'Gladiators' and 'The Krypton Factor'. 'It's the most egotistical and arrogant song I've ever written,' Freddie would often say. The video, directed by Derek Burbridge, was filmed at the New London Theatre – Freddie's choice, for it was here in 1972 that Marlene Dietrich had filmed her one and only television spectacular – and instead of hiring extras to make up an audience, fans were brought in from all over England. After the shoot, as a token of their appreciation, Queen treated them to a complimentary concert.

A few days later Queen were able to sever their ties with Trident completely by buying the 1 per cent royalties' clause in their termination contract. It also emerged that they were experiencing difficulties with their current manager, John Reid, largely because Reid could not handle Elton John and one of the biggest bands in the world and offer both his undivided attention. The severance contract, negotiated by Jim Beach and signed with typical aplomb in the back of Freddie's Rolls-Royce, effected a break which was expedient and amicable, but costly. Henceforth, Reid would exact a hefty 15 per cent royalty on all the albums Queen had released so far, together with an undisclosed, allegedly massive cash settlement – enough of a 'penalty' for the group to opt for self-management from then on.

Over the ensuing months, three limited companies would be set up: Queen Productions, Queen Music and Queen Films. Advised on complicated tax issues by their accountant, the group also formed a fourth company, Rainbow Productions, to handle their overseas revenue which, they were told, would be exempt from British tax so long as they spent no more than sixty-five days of each year in England. They were also advised to record sections of their future albums in different countries to avoid paying performance taxes, which of course saved them a fortune. For their first 'year out', as it is technically known, each member of the group awarded himself a salary of £700,000 – enough for anyone to retire on, as one journalist ridiculously suggested to Freddie, who retorted typically, 'Retire, dear? But what else would I do? I can't cook, and I'm not a very good housewife. I'm just a musical prostitute, dear!'

The group were now able to afford a few luxuries, such as the huge lacquered Japanese piano which Freddie bought in New York, and the private plane Queen hired to commute between venues on their next American tour – the second in less than a year – which opened in Portland on 11 November 1977, a few days after the release of their 'News of the World' album.

Reaching the Top Five on both sides of the Atlantic, and selling over seven million copies worldwide, the album had a sci-fi cover designed by Frank Kelly Freas – an adaptation of a magazine cover he had drawn during the Fifties which depicted the corpses of Brian and Freddie in the clutch of an enormous robot, while Roger and John tumble lifelessly into space. 'News of the World' was possibly their rowdiest, most sensational variation of musical styles so far, though only three of the eleven songs were written by Freddie. The title was, of course, a direct reference to the tabloid attacks of the last few years. The group actually met Freas in Norfolk, Virginia, where they were appearing at the Scope Arena and the Chrysler Museum was holding an exhibition of his work. For Freddie, however, nothing surpassed his meeting with Liza Minelli, on 2 December. Judy Garland's daughter was appearing on Broadway in *The Act*, and Freddie was apparently too shy to ask to meet her after the show. This was rectified after the second of Queen's two concerts at the Madison Square Garden, where Minelli asked to see *him*. On this particular occasion he had received a roisterous welcome by strutting on to the stage wearing a Yankees' baseball strip.

During this tour the American music press treated the group with the respect they had long deserved. Only one concert was not played to a capacity crowd. This was the one in Dayton, Ohio, on 4 December, when adverse weather conditions prevented many fans from getting to the venue, and when it was revealed that the auditorium at the university had a half-inch coating of frost because of heating failure. Even so, the show went ahead and no one was disappointed. Queen's most extravagant performance, Freddie's way of giving fans a good time and reminding Hollywood that he was just as capable as anyone there of organizing an evening to remember, took place at the Los Angeles Forum three days before Christmas. At the end of the show one of the security men stomped on to the stage dressed as Santa Claus – flanked by friends and members of Queen's entourage disguised as Christmas trees, gingerbread men, clowns and reindeers – carrying a large sack out of which popped Freddie to direct the hysterically happy audience through several raucous choruses of *White Christmas*, while fake snow, glitter and pink balloons cascaded from the rafters. And, just to show there were no hard feelings, their ex-manager John Reid danced around the stage dressed as a pixie.

Remarkably, despite the success of their American tour, Queen's next single released there, Brian May's *It's Late*, was an almost total failure and their next British single, John Deacon's gentle *Spread Your Wings*, released on the eve of their European tour, did not even make the Top Thirty.

Europe, thankfully, was another story. Queen were the first popular entertainers to play two consecutive concerts at the Forêt Nationale de Bruxelles and be invited back for a third within the week. On 23/24 April they played the Pavilion de Paris, well known for its tetchy, hard-to-please audiences, and received an unprecedented standing ovation. On 28 April they played the Berliner Deutschlandhalle, and after the show were escorted to a notorious transvestite club, Chez Patachou (*not* to be confused with the famous respectable Parisian nightclub run by the equally famous *chanteuse* of the same name), where the resident dance troupe performed several of their songs in a crude Weimar sketch that even Freddie found surprising. The next day, Brian and Roger crossed Checkpoint Charlie into the city's Eastern sector, John did some sightseeing, and Freddie stayed in his hotel room with a German 'friend', cracking, 'If they get *me* over there, dear, they'll never let me out!'

Returning to England early in May, Queen played just five gigs at two venues – Stafford's Bingley Hall and London's Empire Pool. They had already outlined most of the tracks on their next album, 'Jazz' – the first to be recorded outside Britain – and while Roger and John flew to Switzerland to work on what they had so far in the Mountain Studios, Montreux, Brian stayed put for the birth of his first son, James, in June, before flying with his family to Canada.

Freddie, probably putting his failed project with Eddie Howell down to experience, lingered long enough in England to complete a venture with another friend, the actor-singer Peter Straker, who had appeared in the controversial stage-show 'Hair', and was about to cut an album. 'He was a perfectionist,' Straker reflected. 'His inventiveness, coupled with a meticulous attention to detail, brought me enormous satisfaction. Freddie celebrated his achievements with extravagant and sumptuous gestures, executed with enormous kindness.' Freddie's generosity in this instance was to invest £20,000 of his own money in 'This One's On Me', which EMI released in 1978. Sadly, though Freddie put a lot of energy into promoting the album, enthusing about Straker's finely tuned voice, the album was not the success he had anticipated.

By the end of July 1978 Freddie was working with the rest of the group in Montreux, when a photograph appeared in a French magazine of him swinging from a chandelier at Roger Taylor's twenty-ninth birthday party. This was a pretty tame affair compared with Freddie's own birthday bash, two months later in Nice, where there was a limitless supply of exotic food, drink and cocaine and where at the end of the evening everyone but Freddie, the voyeur, stripped off and dived into the hotel pool.

Nice, too, had brought other pleasurable rewards when, a few weeks before, Freddie had taken time off from the studio to watch the sporting event of the year, the Tour de France, which had passed along the Côte d'Azur, and to spend the night with a young cyclist named Charles who had dropped out of the race with a ham-string injury. It was this exciting experience which inspired the singer to compose *Bicycle Race*, which Queen at once decided would be their next single.

Charles told me, 'Watching the Tour de France go zipping by, Freddie observed how much more exciting the event would have been, had all those muscular young hunks been naked, or at least wearing just jock-straps! He told me what a wonderful video *that* would have made!' To an extent,

Freddie's dream was partially realized when Queen's production company accepted his proposition to hire sixty-five female models to engage in a nude cycle race around Wimbledon Stadium for the promotional video. This was shot under 'very tight security' – though not apparently tight enough to prevent a paparazzi invasion – at a cost of £20,000 on 17 September, by which time Brian May had supplied the very appropriate *Fat Bottomed Girls* for the double-A side due to be released the following month. The bicycles were supplied free by Halfords, who sent Queen Productions a bill for the seats, which had had to be destroyed.

The single, featuring a bum-shot of the winning girl, brought screams of protest from moralists – forcing it to be temporarily withdrawn from the shops until the offending posterior had been clothed in a pair of drawn-on black panties. The music press hated and condemned both songs, the *New Musical Express* going so far as to publish a rear-view of Freddie with the caption, 'Fat Bottomed Queen'. Even so, it reached Number 11 in the charts, by which time Queen were in the middle of another turbulent sell-out tour of the United States.

The tour opened in Dallas on 28 October 1978, and sitting in the audience was Merrill Shindler of *Playgirl*. The 'entertainment for women' magazine had recently published full-frontal shots of Fifties' pop-idol Fabian, along with nude photographs of several top actors and sportsmen and Henry Kissinger, and rather hoped that Freddie might enhance their gallery with a centrefold. For a man for whom blatant exhibitionism was second nature, however, this was going too far. Shindler described the curtain call:

Mercury is the sort of performer who attracts and repels at the same time – sort of like a rock Wayne Newton. On stage he minces and prances about like an epicene Crusader Rabbit – strutting and striking the most outlandish poses in crotch-bulging sequinned tights, then waggling the microphone stand between his thighs and dropping *bons mots* like, 'I'm going to take a little rest now – maybe get a blow job backstage!' Just who will be administering that blow job is anybody's guess, since Freddie is quite willing to explain, 'I'll go to bed with anything – one sex is as good as another.' But for those who might be offended that Mercury is only in rock 'n' roll for the perversity open to him, he also adds, 'My object in life is to make a lot of money and spend it, though these days I tend to spend it before I make it!'

Three days later in New Orleans, jazz capital of the world – a Hallowe'en few of Queen's entourage or the assembled guests would live down for some time – a pre-launch party for 'Jazz' was held in the Imperial Room at the plush Fairmount Hotel. Record company executives were invited from England, France, Germany and the United States – all sharing a mutual financial interest in Queen, but most of them meeting each other for the first time. Among the 400 guests were representatives of the world's press who reported the events of the midnight-till-dawn extravaganza with gusto – most of them coming away from the Fairmount knowing little more about the new album than when they had arrived, but all having participated in the wildest party of the year. There were fire-eaters, exotic dancers and hermaphrodite strippers, naked female mud-wrestlers, Zulu tribesmen, dwarfs and contortionists. Freddie also supplied several 'models' of both sexes, who spent the entire six hours of the party on their knees in a back-room, entertaining the record company executives and some of his friends who had not scored in the conventional way. He told a young female reporter, who looked innocent enough when entering the Fairmount and anything but when leaving, 'Most hotels offer their clients room-service, dear. This one provides lip-service!'

Merill Shindler, describing the bash as 'a Saturday night in Sodom', dictated a running commentary of events for *Playgirl* – only to have the ensuing features heavily censored by the editor. It concluded:

> On the tabletop in front of me is a painfully thin young woman whose sole item of dress is a g-string not much bigger than a 25-cent piece, and stuffed with twenty-dollar bills. There are drag queens in slingbacks and bouffants, and a bevy of 300-pound Samoan women – naked as jaybirds – one of whom has mastered the knack of puffing a cigarette with her vagina. Queen's latest album is called 'Jazz', though there is no jazz on it. As Freddie points out, 'Jazz can mean anything from bullshit to jive to music!' And, by the time you read this column, it will have sold over a million copies, maybe two. And now, back to Queen's party at the Fairmount Hotel. It's a gala affair, an infectious event! *So* infectious that one guest at the next table decides to take off her dress and join the strippers on the tabletops . . .

If the parents of younger, more impressionable Queen fans read any of these reviews, some of them even more explicit than Merrill Shindler's, they could hardly ignore the album itself, for it came with a complementary poster of the naked bicycle girls. This caused few problems in Britain, but in the American Bible Belt there was such a furore that the album was deemed actually pornographic, and banned until the package had been redesigned to incorporate an application form so that fans could send for the poster by mail order. Freddie then decided to give these moralists something to complain about . . . For Queen's two concerts at New York's Madison Square Garden, on 16 and 17 November, he paid twenty naked women to cycle back and forth across the stage.

There were further problems when a religious group

threatened Elektra with legal action over one of the sleeve credits, which read, 'Thunderbolt Courtesy Of God'. This amounted to nothing, however, when Brian May explained that he had stood out in the street in Montreux to tape the thunderstorm which had then been incorporated into the ending of *Dead On Time*. And the controversy naturally only enhanced sales: 'Jazz' reached Number 6 in the *Billboard* album chart and Number 2 in Britain.

5

Just an Alley Creeper . . .

In January 1979 Queen flew to Hamburg to begin their longest tour so far – twenty-eight concerts, including off-circuit towns and cities such as Saarbrucken and Poitiers, and two dates in Yugoslavia. Much of the time Freddie wore an excruciatingly tight harlequin costume, and on one occasion had just performed *Love of My Life* when Chris Taylor, Roger's (straight) roadie walked on to the stage to hand him his maraccas and a glass of water. Freddie introduced him to his 12,000 fans with, 'This is Crystal. He's got a big dick, and he's good in bed!' On another, he closed the proceedings with, 'Thank you, God bless and sweet dreams, you lot of tarts!'

The tour ended with three shows at the Pavilion de Paris. By now some of Queen's British camp followers – Freddie called them the Royal Family – had begun tinkling bicycle bells as a means of requesting the group's two bicycle numbers, and for some reason this irked French fans, who tolerated the practice until halfway through the third show, when they began fighting. When several of Queen's road crew joined in the fracas, the local *gendarmerie* alerted the riot-squad, who invaded the venue with batons and tear-gas.

At the time of the tour Queen were shortlisted to compose the music for the comic-strip adventure film, *Flash Gordon*. The Italian-born producer, Dino de Laurentiis, was dubious about taking them on, barking impatiently at a meeting with his backers, 'Queen? Never heard of 'em. Who the hell are *they*?' Persuaded to listen to 'A Night at the Opera', however, de Laurentiis very quickly agreed to a commission.

Freddie was in his element, working and improvising in front of the giant screen while the eponymous hero, played by Sam J Jones, swashbuckled towards glory in high-camp fashion. 'Relentlessly smirky, decadent and homoerotic', was how the completed film was reviewed by Paul Roen, in his *High Camp: A Gay Guide to Camp and Cult Films*. 'It's extremely gay, mainly due to the costuming, or in some cases the *lack* of costuming, and combines the dregs of Seventies disco culture with the chauvinistic cruelty of nascent Reaganism.' 'Great fun, providing you ignore the plot and concentrate on the corny performances and cheesy special effects,' was film critic Barry Norman's opinion.

Neither did it go unobserved by Freddie that Jones, an ethereal-looking, dyed-blond, muscular six-footer had first gained recognition when he had bared his considerable assets for a *Playgirl* centrefold. Subsequently, when he learned that four years earlier Dino de Laurentiis had directed an emotive remake of the classic horror movie, *King Kong* – one which had been absolutely panned by the critics – he told a friend, 'Dino made *King Kong*. Now it's my greatest ambition to make it with King Dong!' His plans were scuppered, however, when one of Sam J Jones's pals informed him that the actor was 'not that way'.

Each of Queen's 1979 European concerts was taped to enable the edited, remixed highlights to be incorporated into the double album, 'Live Killers', which was pieced together at Musicland Studios, in Munich. Released in June, it peaked at Number 3 in the charts, surprising the group's record company, for by this time the market was flooded with bootleg tapes, many of them of equal if not better quality than the official release – which had been publicly condemned by Roger Taylor. At around this time, too, Queen bought Mountain Studios, situated on the shores of the picturesque Lake Geneva – a strange move, for in these early, reckless years Freddie often claimed that he could not stand the tranquillity, declaring that the studio should have been under the lake rather than next to it.

In April Queen flew to Japan to an even more riotous welcome than in their first visit four years previously, and as with Europe, there were off-circuit concerts in Kanazawa and Sapporo. Also, this time the Japanese had an 'anthem' of their own. *Teo Toriatte (Let Us Cling Together)*, written by Brian for inclusion in 'A Day at the Races', had a chorus which the group sang in Japanese. By now, however, Freddie was beginning to tire of the way these mostly teenage fans would react giddily throughout each and every song. 'There used to be a time when I loved all this teenybop screaming,' he said. 'But now I think I would perfer them to *listen* to what we're playing.'

Then it was back to Mountain Studios, where Queen began working on their new album, which, in effect, would not be released until the following summer. For Freddie, this was a period of considerable contentment. He loved working with the irascible German engineer, Reinhardt Mack, so much so that Mack was very soon being credited as 'co-producer', and henceforth would play a vital role in the Queen empire, now that the group had dispensed with the services of the hitherto indispensable Roy Thomas Baker.

Freddie fell for Munich in a big way, and for several years the city became his second home. Since his first visit to Germany way back in 1973, he had admired the country's liberated attitude towards homosexuality and the opportunity this had given him to explore a budding sexuality which was now in full decadent bloom. Like post-Stonewall New York, Munich in the Seventies was a hotbed of gay culture where one could sample openly the delights of a wide range of clubs, cinemas, cafés and bars, without fear of disapproval or criticism from so-called straight society. Freddie's nocturnal pilgrimages into the area known as the Bermuda Triangle often saw him accompanied by friends–factotums Joe 'Liza' Fanelli, Peter 'Phoebe' Freestone and Paul Prenter. Afterwards there would be wild parties in Roger Taylor's hotel suite – the 'HH', or 'Heterosexual Hangout' – and even wilder ones in the suite Freddie was sharing with his pals – the 'PPP', or 'Presidential Pouffes' Parlour'.

Casting what few inhibitions he had to the wind, Freddie did exactly what he liked, where and when the mood took him. He was justifiably proud of the photograph which appeared in a German gay magazine. Wearing his now famous harlequin costume, he is seen smooching on the dance-floor with a young man who is sporting an undersized silk bomber-jacket, and nothing else.

In next to no time Freddie was rubbing shoulders with the likes of Amanda Lear, Helmut Berger, gay porn star Peter Berlin and film-director Rainer Werner Fassbinder, the undisputed champion of sado-masochistic sex, alcohol and drugs whose behaviour made that of his most lascivious contemporaries appear tame. Although Freddie confessed that Fassbinder was 'not his cup of char', he did admire the odd-looking director for bravely tackling the subject of homosexuality in his work and for attracting rave reviews from critics renowned for their homophobia. He was equally fascinated by three of Fassbinder's leading ladies, whom he met at the notorious New York Bar: Hanna Schygulla, Ingrid Caven and Barbara Valentin. He told a German reporter, 'I love Schygulla's ice-cool acting style, and Caven reminds me of a cross between Piaf and Dietrich when she sings.

Valentin, dear, fascinates me because she's got such great tits!'

All three stars, of course, like the icons they have emulated or paid tribute to over the last twenty years, had huge homosexual followings across Europe and were referred to by patrons of the seedy Frisco Bar, another favourite Mercury haunt, somewhat ingloriously as 'The Three Fag-Hags'. Of the three, however, it was Valentin who attracted him the most and their friendship developed into a close bonding, not unlike Freddie's relationship with Mary Austin – so much so that when they began living together, rumours ran rife that Freddie was about to become 'Mr Valentin Number Four'. Reinhardt Mack actually said in an interview that Freddie's gayness was perfectly dispensable – to the effect that he would have 'grown' out of it given an opportunity to sire children, and bearing in mind that he loved women! The statement has since been dismissed by Freddie's close friends as flippant and ridiculous. One told me:

> Although Freddie could have married and made a wonderful father, he was never, *never* a hypocrite and could never have sworn to stay faithful or change his ways. He was sublimely happy the way he was. And being gay isn't an illness. You can't suddenly decide you're cured and go from being one way to the other.

Many years later, yet another Queen spokesperson who chose to remain anonymous told the *Daily Mirror* that Freddie only lived with the two women in his life so that his mother would not ask too many awkward questions about his sexuality – a statement which makes one wonder how, with all the scurrilous tabloid stories and Freddie's outrageous comments she could *not* have known the truth. It is also an incontestable fact that while Freddie and Valentin were sleeping together, this relationship was entirely different from the one with Mary Austin because they were usually sleeping on either side of some young man either or both of them had picked up at one of Munich's countless rough-trade joints. Admitting she and Freddie often bashed each other whenever jealousy reared its ugly head, which was often, the busty actress said, 'We had *exactly* the same taste in men. Our favourites were big-all-over truck-driver types. We couldn't get enough of them!' Another of his German lovers, Kurt, revealed Freddie's 'demoralization process', whereby if a man tried to act too butch in the bedroom, he would be brought down a peg or two by being assigned to the role of one of Freddie's film heroines:

> Freddie was absolutely crazy about Gloria Swanson. I was just twenty, and didn't even know who she was. He asked me to take off all my clothes, which I did *most* willingly . . . Then he plonked this huge, old-fashioned hat on my head, a mass of smelly feathers which he said Swanson had worn in *Sunset Boulevard*. Then he rushed downstairs to give me my cue. He yelled cut, and I descended the staircase as he improvised a scene from *Whatever Happened to Baby Jane?* Then he absolutely *howled* with laughter. Someone told me afterwards that Freddie did this sort of thing to humiliate his lovers, but I don't think so. He was such a kind, gentle man and I would do absolutely anything, now, just to hear that wonderful laugh of his once more.

On 18 August 1979 Queen made a return trip to Saarbrucken, to top the bill at an open-air festival in the 32,000-capacity Ludwigparkstadion. This time Roger was the centre of attention when he walked on to the stage sporting green hair – the result of a last-minute bid to bleach his hair. The concert was beset with technical problems from start to finish – and by the end of it, Taylor's frustration got the better of him and he smashed his drumkit to pieces.

Early in October Queen released their single, *Crazy Little Thing Called Love*, one of the four songs recorded in Munich. It was a bouncy rockabilly number, penned by Freddie in his bath, and one which would not have been out of place in Elvis Presley's later repertoire. 'It isn't typical of my work,' Freddie counteracted, ahead of the critics who would lampoon it. 'But that's only because nothing ever *is* typical of my work!' The record quickly reached Number 2 in the British charts – a far cry from their last single, a live version of *Love of My Life*, which had stalled at Number 63, and it gave Queen their first American Number One. The video, additionally, was tremendous fun, an innocuous promotion of homoeroticism tinged with Benny-Hill-style humour: a leather-clad Queen, with a brialliantined, knee-padded Freddie being forcibly dragged on to the catwalk by two muscular hunks, before being groped by a bevvy of busty lovelies in suspenders, one of which sensually blows smoke into the camera while another proceeds to rip Freddie's T-shirt from top to bottom.

When first screened on 'Top of the Pops', the video brought an unexpected outburst from Rob Halford, the lead singer with the leather-and-chains hard-rock ensemble, Judas Priest, who accused Queen of 'purloining' their image. Halford threw down the gauntlet, challenging Freddie to 'prove his machismo' by using the huge motorcycle he had straddled in the film to race him around the circuit at Brands Hatch. 'Fine,' Freddie barked, adding with reference to his next project, 'so long as the gentleman agrees to do a *pas-de-deux* with the Royal Ballet!' Needless to say, the challenge was soon withdrawn.

Crazy Little Thing Called Love was chosen by Freddie, along with *Bohemian Rhapsody*, for his special charity performance with the Royal Ballet, on 7 October at the London Coliseum. A keen ballet enthusiast, he had attended many of the company's performances and was a close friend of principal dancer Wayne Eagling. 'Sadly, not close enough,' he lamented to one friend. 'I mean, how can anyone as gorgeous as that be *straight*? Mind you, dear, I *did* get a peep at what goes inside those tights!'

The Coliseum show was to raise funds for the Society For Handicapped Children, and Eagling and his colleague, Derek Dane, put Freddie through his paces for the two dances they had especially choreographed. It was one of the toughest ordeals of his career, but, wearing a silver-spangled all-in-one open at the front to expose the now obligatory dense expanse of chest hair, he performed each step perfectly, receiving a roisterous standing ovation from hundreds of ballet afficionados who would never have even dreamed of listening to a Queen record. However, as with 'Live Killers', Roger Taylor voiced his opinion, upsetting Freddie by dismissing the evening as 'dreadful'.

At the party in the Crush Bar after the show, Freddie was introduced to one of the charity's patrons, Prince Andrew, and lost no time at all breaking the ice. The fun-loving royal was attempting to eat a dish of strawberries, when Freddie screeched at the top of his voice, 'Phoebe, take it away!' 'Phoebe' was Peter Freestone, the ballet company's wardrobe assistant, whom Freddie would poach as his new *chevalier servant* before the evening was through. While they were chatting, the fringe of Freddie's scarf dropped into his drink. When Prince Andrew politely wrung it out, Freddie quipped, 'Thank goodness you've put me at my ease. Now I can use the odd bit of dirty language!' Then, when asked if he was going to sing one of the prince's favourite songs – he never got around to saying what this was – Freddie issued an ultimatum. He would sing, providing Andrew agreed to swing from one of the chandeliers and to accompany him and a few friends for a jar at Heaven, the gay disco-club near Charing Cross.

The first request was denied, though Prince Andrew did agree to the club date. 'Mr Mercury's party were escorted to a private, very discreet table,' the then manager explained.

'They did not get up to dance, but drank, laughed and chattered until the early hours of the morning.'

At the end of November 1979 Queen embarked on what they would label their 'Crazy Tour' – an alternative schedule of venues much smaller than the ones they had been playing in recent years, in order to establish a more intimate contact between themselves and their audiences. Unfortunately, this caused monstrous problems with security, and with the police who each evening were faced with the possibility of a riot among fans who, unable to purchase tickets, turned up anyway hoping for a miracle with touts. There was even talk of some shows being cancelled altogether. The worst that happened, however, was a last-minute cancellation of the group's in-store signing at HMV's Oxford Street shop, on 12 December .

The tour opened in Dublin, where Freddie stole the show with a heart-rending arangement of *The Londonderry Air* – in direct contrast to his curtain-call, for which he was carried on to the stage on the shoulders of a minder dressed as Superman. It closed at the Alexandra Palace, three days before Christmas, with a very noisy *We Will Rock You*, during which Freddie danced across the stage, pelting the audience with bananas, something he had seen his friend Divine do during one of his early cabaret performances in New York. On Boxing Day Queen played a charity gig at the Hammersmith Odeon – the first in a series employing different stars each evening, organized by Paul McCartney in aid of war-torn Kampuchea.

There was also a new regular man in Freddie's life. After Queen's 10 December concert at the Brighton Centre Freddie, Paul Prenter and a few others had retreated to one of the resort's most popular gay spots, the Curtain Club. Here, he had ended up dancing cheek-to-cheek with a handsome, moustachioed twenty-eight-year-old courier named Tony Bastin. The pair spent that night in Freddie's hotel suite, and the singer is said to have fallen for him in a big way – certainly enough to warrant Bastin relocating to Freddie's flat, along with his beautiful ginger tom, Oscar, who some years later Freddie would claim as his own, long after he had stopped loving the man.

After the tour Bastin formed part of Queen's entourage when they returned to Munich to resume work on their new studio album, 'The Game', and to work some more on the *Flash Gordon* soundtrack. 'The Game', of course, was an apt title for a group which seemed to be persistently in competition with itself, as Brian May later explained, 'We were always trying to take the next step – a million records this year, two million next. One night at Madison Square Garden this time, two next time. It's like being at school – get better marks and get a pat on the head. It was artificial, a game, a very comforting game.'

The guitarist also admitted that he and the other members of the group often fought among themselves in the studio, adding, 'We'd hate each other for a while and get very angry with each other. I left the group a couple of times – just for the day, you know. "I'm off and I'm not coming back!" You end up quibbling over one note.' More serious were the arguments about money, particularly over the dissention caused by Roger Taylor earning the same royalties for his composition on the B-side of *Bohemian Rhapsody* as Freddie had earned for Queen's most celebrated song, though Freddie does not appear to have been too concerned about this, quipping, 'Four cocks fighting – how nice!'

At around this time Freddie changed his 'tinsel and glitter' image, the object of so much scorn from his detractors. Throwing away his nail varnish and mascara, he cropped short his beautiful long hair and grew a bushy moustache. 'It's a growth process,' he said. 'People grow up. After ten or twelve years you have to be seen to be growing up, and the people who've grown up with you can't suddenly say, "My God, he's still got long hair, and he's still wearing black

Mad about the boy. (*Redferns*)

'Home? I don't wanna go home.' (*Redferns*)

'*D'amor sull'ali rosee.*' (*Bret/Cinemago, Paris*)

'In the wake of the human tornado.' (*Bret/Cinemago, Paris*)

Scorpio rising. (*Redferns*)

'All I have to do is throw my carcass around the stage.' (*Redferns*)

'I am what I am, so is a stone, them that don't like me can leave me alone.' (*Redferns*)

'I still love you.' (*Redferns*)

fingernails and a lady's blouse!" I mean, it's ridiculous, and I would *feel* ridiculous!'

This 'new' Freddie made his début in the video for Queen's new single, *Play the Game* – their first song to have incorporated synthesizers, a fine boast – which was released in May. His change of appearance brought screams of disapproval from female and straight fans, particularly in the United States, but sighs of ecstasy from gay ones, particularly when Freddie suddenly began appearing 'topless', baring an expanse of chest hair and flexing a more than generous set of muscles – a far cry from his 'Bo-Rap' days. Over the next few months thousands of Freddie clones would begin flocking to discos across the world.

Queen's ninth album, 'The Game', was released at the end of June 1980, and went straight to the top of the charts – not that this prevented it from being attacked almost unanimously by the music press. Only *Sounds* seems to have truly appreciated it and recognized its worth, hailing it as 'A straight kick into the goal . . . like winning the Men's Singles at Wimbledon'. The latter comment alluded to an idea floated by Queen the previous summer that they should give an out-of-season concert in the All England Club's revered Centre Court, a suggestion which was very quickly nipped in the bud by the club's officials.

'Play the Game' attracted a great deal of heated criticism from a small section of overzealous fans who accused Queen of selling them short, in breaking their promise, made back in 1973, never to use synthesizers, and now going back on their word and heading in the same direction as their less-worthy contemporaries. All was well, however, when a group spokesman issued a statement to the effect that Queen were merely keeping abreast with modern technology – and in any case, their input of gadgetry was so minuscule that, rather than interfere with their instrument-playing, it only served to enhance it.

There were further, more light-hearted protests a few days later when Queen embarked on a gruelling, forty-six-day sell-out tour of North America. Still outraged by Freddie's new image, some fans pelted the stage with razors, packs of razor blades and plastic bottles of nail varnish.

The new look, however, opened new doors for Freddie's already considerable sexual appetite when the group arrived in Los Angeles to give four concerts at the Forum. Indeed, Paul Prenter later emphasized that Freddie had changed his appearance in the first place only so that he would be able to attract more of the butch-looking, hirsute men he had always preferred. One of the first of this new breed was John Murphy, a thirty-year-old airline steward from Los Angeles whom Freddie had met during the flight from London to New York. Their affair would be brief, though long enough for Freddie's eyes to be opened one evening after Queen's show, when Murphy and a group of leather enthusiasts took him on a foray into the seamier side of the city's gay scene. They took in such landmarks as the I-Beam, where tank-tops were still the rage, and the Black & Blue, where motorcycles were suspended from the rafters and many of the clientele turned up in full bondage-gear for the six-hour 'fuckathon' which was advertised in all the local contact magazines, and which began on the stroke of midnight when the doors of the establishment were closed to all but its regulars.

The Black & Blue, however, was pretty tame compared with the Glory Holes (aka South of Market Club), where Freddie met one of his idols, Rock Hudson, only recently out of the closet and desperately afraid of being recognized. Although Freddie and Hudson were definitely not each other's types – the actor always had a penchant for muscular blonds, and Freddie almost without exception preferred what David Evans termed, 'Nice, well-built people with a good lot of meat on them' – this did not prevent them from engaging in a little harmless, mutual observation.

Brought to the world's attention via the novels of

Armistead Maupin, the Glory Holes consisted of several bars and any number of plywood booths, each with several holes, through which customers would insert their penises in anticipation of gratification from the other side. But if the recipient never knew at the time who was 'pleasuring' him, the hundreds of men assembled on the balcony which overlooked the booths were able to observe and applaud every movement. Both Freddie and Rock Hudson were offered membership of the Glory Holes but, much to the relief of their friends and entourages, both declined.

During this American tour 'The Game' became Queen's first Stateside Number One, and one of its tracks – John Deacon's *Another One Bites the Dust* – shot to the top of the singles charts, where it remained for five weeks, selling three million copies and bringing their sales totals, to date, to thirty million singles and twice as many albums, and enabling the *Guinness Book of Records* to place them at the top of its 'World's Richest Directors' segment. In England the single reached Number 7, and like *We Are The Champions* became a stadium anthem – aimed at the losing side, of course. The song also allowed Queen access to yet another new musical style, funk, until then almost exclusive to black disco artists.

Hot on the heels of this success, in November 1980, *Flash* was released as a single, taken from the *Flash Gordon* soundtrack album which hit the shops on 8 December. The record made the Top Ten in Britain, but barely scraped into the American Top Fifty. Though by no means one of Queen's best songs, it was unusual in that it broke new ground as a novelty item, cleverly incorporating snatches of dialogue from the film, lots of thunderflashes – besides taking a risk by not featuring Freddie on lead vocals.

Early in December, after a brief spell in Europe, Queen were the first act to play the newly built 11,000-seater Birmingham New Exhibition Centre, where over two evenings 22,000 fans heard some of the *Flash Gordon* songs for the first time, synthesizers-et-al. To highlight the sci-fi element of their set, Freddie was carried on stage on the shoulders of his burly minder, who was dressed as Darth Vadar. Because the group had thought it unnecessary to seek permission to use the name and image of the *Star Wars* character as a publicity ploy, this breach of copyright saw them served with a writ which, though irksome, eventually came to nothing.

The focal point of the evening, however, was Freddie's German leather shorts – some of his entourage began taking bets as to whether they would 'contain' him until the end of the show. They did, and afterwards he barked at an attendant reporter, 'Thank goodness I didn't get a hard-on, dear, otherwise I would have ended up singing like Yma Sumac!'

This was also Freddie's British fans' first glimpse of his new image, of which James Johnson of the *Evening Standard* disapproved. 'He *has* dropped some of his overtly camp affectations,' Johnson wrote. 'But a new moustache suggests he is looking for a spare-time job as a waiter in the Fulham Road.'

This flying visit to Britain, however, did become tinged with tragedy when on 9 December, the day of their second of three concerts at Wembley Arena, Queen were informed of the death of John Lennon, fatally shot by a lunatic fan named Mark Chapman outside his New York apartment at around 5.00 a.m. British time. The group at once decided to pay tribute to the man who, it is claimed, had been spurred into making a recent comeback only after listening to *Crazy Little Thing Called Love*.

With only hours to spare, Queen put together a special arrangement of Lennon's theme for peace, *Imagine*. Such was the emotion that halfway through, Brian May began playing the wrong chord and Freddie, choking back the tears, forgot the words. It was one of the rare occasions that he ever faltered on stage.

*

In February 1981, Queen played five sell-out concerts at the Tokyo Budokan, and at the end of the month embarked on their greatest risk so far, a tour of South America. Barring several megatours by Latin stars Amália Rodrigues, Celia Cruz and Julio Iglesias, this part of the world had never hosted any mass concerts and indeed had no idea how to organize a technical extravaganza – the lighting-rig alone of which demanded 300,000 watts of power – the like of Queen's, let alone supply a suitably sized venue.

Dubbed the 'Gluttons for Punishment' tour, the event required three months of forward planning, and an estimated budget of £¾ million, added to which were the group's collective expenses of £25,000 a *day* once they hit the road. On top of this was the cost of supplying several tons of Astroturf to cover the 'hallowed' pitch of Buenos Aires' famous Velez Sarsfield soccer stadium, and of redesigning the tour logo – a pair of naked ladies, one of which was holding a banana suggestively – on account of South America's stringent laws against pornography . . . laws which were so draconian that when a group of male fans opted to impersonate Freddie by strolling quite innocuously through the city streets wearing shorts which by his standards would not even have been regarded as skimpy, they were promptly arrested, charged with gross public indecency, and jailed for two days.

Queen's arrival at Buenos Aires airport on 23 February was tantamount to them having been given the freedom of the city – hardly surprising, perhaps, owing to the fact that every one of their albums was in the Argentinian Top Ten. For thirty minutes flights were delayed as the intercom system broadcast Queen songs, and they were officially welcomed into a politically unsound Argentina by a presidential aide. Because of a strong terrorist element which had threatened to infiltrate the group's Spanish–Portuguese entourage, this official presence was a warning to would-be insurrectionists who had earlier protested about the 'capitalism' of a rock concert in a country which was rife with poverty. Subsequently, they were accompanied virtually everywhere by a squad of machine-gun-toting military police. Freddie made light of this, posing for photographs with these hunky chaps and enthusing, 'All that meat and leather. Why don't you come to dinner tonight, dears?' He was perhaps surprised when several of them accepted the invitation – even more so at the end of the evening when, after toasting him with champagne, they tore off their official insignia and presented it to the group.

Queen's Buenos Aires concert on 28 February was filmed and broadcast the next evening to forty million viewers throughout Argentina and Brazil. It ended with the British and Argentinian flags being unfurled at opposite ends of the stadium. Afterwards, the group were invited to a party at the home of the country's football manager, where they met one of their biggest fans, the legendary footballer Diego Maradona, who posed for photographs with the group in the Union Jack T-shirt which Freddie had given him. Freddie's shirt, as he playfully pointed out to everyone, bore the 'Le Coq' logo.

The next day, the group were invited to an audience with President Viola, which brought the speedy response from Freddie, 'How nice for them to have named a president after a pansy!' He was, however, said to have been angry at Roger Taylor's abrupt refusal of Viola's such obviously put-on generosity, 'We came over here to sing to the people, not to meet politicians.'

Following concerts at huge stadia in Mar del Plata and Rosario, and a return to the Velez Sarsfield which saw them all but beatified, Queen moved on to Brazil, where their promoter lost the battle to get them permission to perform at the Maracoña Stadium in Rio de Janeiro, owing to a recent law forbidding the country's stadia from being used for anything other than sporting or religious events. Even the offer of a phenomenally huge donation towards the

Governor of Rio's favourite charity failed to cut any ice, however, and the group enjoyed the sights and pleasures of the city until 20/21 March, when they reluctantly staged two concerts at the Morumbi Stadium, in São Paulo, each evening to a world-record-breaking 130,000 people, few of whom understood a word of English, while still capable of belting out every word of *Love of My Life*. To avoid the Brazilians' insistence that PA systems had to be stripped down and searched for contraband – an immensely time-consuming operation which resulted in a great deal of equipment being left in the country (which the wily Brazilians sometimes promptly rented out again) – immediately after their second show, while it was still dark and the South American promoter was busy filching the artificial turf from the stadium, Queen's one hundred tons of equipment were secreted into a juggernaut, then smuggled on to a private cargo-plane and flown out of the country.

Queen spent most of the summer in Munich, working on their next album, 'Hot Space', and generally living life to the full in their favourite location, enjoying a seemingly endless succession of all-night raves which saw them more often than not staggering into the studio bleary-eyed, but nevertheless producing their best work for some time. Roger Taylor followed the same theme too by releasing his début solo album, 'Fun in Space', which reached the Top Twenty, though the singles from it flopped. 'He can *write* the songs,' observed *Sounds*, some time later when Taylor was still churning out chart failures, 'but he can't sing them like Freddie, which is why *Queen* get the hits.'

Much more fruitful was Queen's project with David Bowie, who lived close to the Mountain Studios in Montreux. Bowie had dropped in on one of their rehearsal sessions a while before, resulting in an impromptu jam-session which had produced at least one song, *People in the Streets*, though recording with Bowie, according to Brian May, had been much less pleasurable. He told an American press conference a few years later, 'David was aloof in the studio. He's a perfectionist. Working with him was a very difficult experience.'

Changed to *Under Pressure*, this very un-Queenlike duet would be released as a single at the end of October 1981, and not surprisingly go straight to Number 1. Because Bowie and Queen were working in different parts of the world, however, and were unable to get together for a video, David Mallett was instructed to let his imagination run wild. This he did, compiling a 'stress' tapestry of mostly vintage film footage: tube station chaos, Nosferatu the vampire, collapsing tower blocks, the Wall Street Crash, poverty, soup kitchens and mass unemployment, assuaged by Hollywood kisses from Garbo, John Gilbert and Valentino. The video was banned by the BBC, however, because it contained footage of IRA bombings in Belfast.

On 5 September Freddie began celebrating his thirty-fifth birthday in his huge rented suite in New York's plush Berkshire Hotel. Determined this time to be more flamboyant and outrageous than ever, he flew a hundred of his closest friends in from London – on Concorde at £3,000 a throw – telling them, 'Don't worry about the cost, dears. The only thing you'll have to pay for will be the condoms!' Other friends were invited from his favourite gay clubs, including the regulars and a few 'turns' from the notorious Mineshaft, an establishment which catered for enthusiasts of sado-masochism, and which Freddie had recently designated his 'most cherished American den of iniquity' since the Glory Holes along with many New York and San Francisco saunas and bath-houses had been forcibly closed because of what was described by one tabloid as 'A mysterious, influenza-type malady which for some inexplicable reason is picking off only members of the gay community'. Freddie called his friends from the Mineshaft his 'New York gals', and rewarded each and every one of them for attending his party with a solid gold Cartier wristwatch.

On 25 September Queen went on stage at the Poliedro de Caracas, in Venezuala, the opening date in the second leg of their South America tour. Here, political unrest was particularly acute. The former president, Romulo Ethancourt, hailed as 'The Father Of Democracy', was critically ill, and rumours that a revolution would erupt were he not to survive were rife. The group played three of their five proposed concerts, and all seemed well. Then, on 28 September, Ethancourt died, plunging the entire country into a week-long period of mourning during which virtually everything shut down, preventing Queen and their crew from leaving the country. There were further problems when the latter eventually attempted to cross the border into Mexico. Due to restrictions on the issue of visas, they were held up for several days – until the border guards were bribed to let them through. If this was not enough, one week later – after Queen's triumphant show in Monterrey – the local promoter, José Rota, was arrested and sent to jail and the group were compelled to put up the $25,000 to get him released – something they would not have done had they been able to see into the very near future.

Prior to Queen's two concerts in Puebla, their fans were rough-handled by security, who relieved them of any alcohol they were trying to smuggle in, then removed the films from their cameras and the batteries from their tape-recorders . . . only to pass this contraband to the merchandise stalls within the stadium, which sold everything back at three times its original cost. Many of them reacted by pelting the stage with empty bottles, coins and even shoes, and Paul Prenter was hit in the face with a battery. The last straw, however, came when José Rota informed the group that their fee for the second Puebla show was to be confiscated for tax reasons. Instead of moving on to Guadalajara for their next concert, Queen flew to New York, leaving their promoter and thousands of fans in the lurch, and swearing that they would never set foot in Mexico again.

At the end of November Queen were invited to play two concerts at the 18,000-seater Montreal Forum. These were filmed, with the intention of turning the footage into a full-length feature film to be premièred in cinemas throughout North America during the summer of 1982, then put on general release in Britain and most of Europe. The project – directed by Saul Swimmer, the man responsible for the Beatles' *Let It Be* – was plagued with problems, mainly financial, from its conception. Fortunately for Queen's fans, but more especially for their detractors, this badly edited, poorly synchronized mish-mash did not see the light of day until 1984, when it was released as a video, *We Will Rock You*. In November 1981, however, Queen were riding majestically on their highest wave. The single with Bowie was at Number 1, as was their first compilation album, 'Greatest Hits', and its accompanying video, *Greatest Flix* – not just in Britain, but throughout most of the world.

It was, however, the little things that touched Freddie's heart – the fact that Queen were so big that when an American fan sent a letter addressed simply to 'Queen – England', it ended up at Buckingham Palace, whereupon the real Queen's comptroller fowarded it to them with the apology, 'Opened in error.'

6

Never Wanted to Be the Boy Next Door

Queen's music was officially blessed by the classical world when, on 8 December 1981, the Royal Philharmonic Orchestra and Choir played a concert of their songs at London's Royal Albert Hall. All the proceeds, including royalties from the subsequent album and video sales, were donated to leukaemia research.

The group themselves spent much of the early part of 1982 in Munich, adding the finishing touches to 'Hot Space'. In April they released a new single, *Body Language*, c/w *Life is Real*, their belated studio tribute to John Lennon. From the fans' point of view – many of whom had given John Deacon's new funky sound a very definite thumbs down – the single and the subsequent album were the worst of Queen's reign and almost cost them their crown, reaching only Number 25 and Number 4 in their respective charts.

The single fared much better in America because of its promotional video featuring naked bodies smeared in baby oil, which sparked off a controversy when parents of younger fans denounced it as 'lewd' and petitioned the record company to change it. In South Africa the single was denounced as 'immoral' and banned completely.

Freddie was always the first to admit a preference for one-night stands, or even flings lasting just a few hours, in spite of his regrets in later life that there had been but a handful of lovers who had been special. According to some reports he was not always the nicest of men, particularly when crossed. A few days after Freddie's death, an EMI executive spoke of the incident in the back of the star's limousine which occurred on the outskirts of Munich, during the late spring of 1982. 'We were trying to snort coke and watch the television at the same time,' the executive said. 'Then, Freddie's latest man switched channels, and he went bonkers, shouting and screaming. He told the driver to stop the car, then physically kicked the guy out into the road, leaving him stranded miles from anywhere. Then we went and found Freddie a new friend.'

The new friend, who would replace Tony Bastin as Freddie's regular lover, was a dark-haired, moustachioed young restaurateur named Winnie Kirkenberger, who actually dated him for several days before realizing who he was. And even after that, he refused to succumb to the privileged treatment which went hand-in-glove with being *chevalier servant* to one of the world's biggest rock stars, though he did accept a 'little gift' . . . a brand-new Mercedes 560.

Freddie and Kirkenberger would remain lovers throughout most of the singer's sojourn in Munich, though they were never faithful to each other. Over the next three years there would be countless three- and even four-in-a-bed scenarios, frequently drugs- and drink-enhanced. At this time Freddie is said to have been spending upwards of £1,000 a week on vodka and cocaine just for his personal use. Paul Prenter spoke of an amusing occasion when, *en route* from New York to London on Concorde, Freddie discovered half a gram of cocaine in his shoulder-bag and, rather than be caught with it by customs officials at Heathrow, he decided to snort it there and then in his seat. 'After that, Freddie could have flown home by himself,' Prenter mused.

A row erupted in June, as Queen were coming towards the end of a European tour and the Falklands War was reaching its zenith. *Under Pressure* was Number One in Argentina, and radio stations around the world were broadcasting one of their latest songs, *Las Palabras De Amor*, recorded as a tribute to their many thousands of South American fans. The fact that some of the lyrics were in Spanish was regarded as insensitive by opponents of the Argentinian dictator, President Galtieri, while the mere title of the duet with Bowie was declared 'propagandist' by him. Galtieri subsequently issued a decree banning all Queen's records from being played over the air, but allowing them to be sold in the shops because they needed the revenue, and the group were told that they would never be allowed into Argentina again. This upset Freddie deeply. Several of his Argentine one-night stands had since been recruited into military service and, completely a-political and regardless of the fact that he probably would never see them again, he was still concerned for their well-being. He told the press, 'This silly conflict is all about our young men killing *their* young men. Where's the *glory* in being blown to bits?'

In 1982 there would be just four British concerts, Queen's first in eighteen months: two in Edinburgh, one at Leeds' Elland Road, and one at the recently constructed Milton Keynes Bowl. Two others were cancelled: one at the Arsenal football stadium because it was unable to obtain a live events licence, and the one at Old Trafford because of a shortage of portable toilets, which had all been commandeered by arguably the most important tour of the year, that of the Pope.

The Milton Keynes show on 5 June was filmed by Tyne Tees Television. It was broadcast on the first edition of Channel 4's 'The Tube' on 7 January 1983, and proved to be a suitable anodyne to the disappointing *We Will Rock You* video. Freddie, in fine vocal form and ruder than usual – at one stage of the concert he proferred his posterior to the audience, and several times 'masturbated' his microphone stand – belied the fact that he was probably still suffering from the shakes after a hair-raising flight to the venue, his first in a helicopter. Time and time again he leapt on to the scaffolding, balancing precariously, high over the heads of the audience.

After this show Queen paid £100,000 to hire London's Embassy Club for a 'shorts-and-suspenders' party. One of the guests was Diana Ross, whom Freddie had worshipped since her days with the Supremes, and he was in such a hurry to get to the bash that, mindless of his terror, he agreed to another helicopter trip. There was, however, a last-minute hitch. Freddie arrived late, after an impatient Ross had already left.

From mid-July until September, Queen toured the United States and Canada. A notable event occurred on 23 July when the Mayor of Boston awarded them the keys to the city. On 25 September the group made their first and only live American appearance, on 'Saturday Night Live', when Freddie accompanied himself on the guitar and offered a more than passable imitation of Elvis Presley with a rollicking *Crazy Little Thing Called Love*.

In October they paid another visit to Japan. Their final show there, at the Seibu Lions Stadium in Tokyo, was filmed and fourteen songs were later released on a commercial Japanese-system-only video. All in all it was a busy year, with seventy huge, extremely costly extravaganzas in twelve countries – in effect their heaviest schedule in five years.

But if fans were expecting more of the same over the next twelve months, they were in for a disappointment: at the end of 1982 the group announced that they would be taking six months off, maybe even a year. A combination of fatigue, the relative failure (compared with their other albums, that is) of 'Hot Space', but above all artistic temperament had begun taking its toll.

For the music press, who had been sounding the death-knell for as long as anyone cared to remember, the fact that Queen might this time have really come to the end of their particular road was manna from heaven, though Freddie was very much on the defensive. Admitting that all their clashes centred around their oversized egos, and the fact that each member of the group more often than not wrote his contribution to a song while apart from the others, he told *Rockline*:

> Sometimes I'll take one of my songs to Brian and he may put guitars on *my* song the way *he* wants to, not my way. So we'll fight. Sometimes we're the bitchiest band in the world! There's a lot of bad vibes, but in the end it always comes together. We *have* to fight, otherwise it would be a bit boring!

And on the matter of Queen's split, he explained to the *Baghdad Observer*:

> Some of us enjoy making solo albums, but we *love* getting together as a band and there is the obvious question: why kill the goose that lays the golden eggs? Okay, so we won't be running around the stage when we're forty-five. That would be silly. But, if we *do* split up – well, dear, I suppose I'll just have to go off and become a striptease artist!

For the first seven months of the year, the four members of the group were content to go their separate ways. John Deacon devoted himself to his growing family. Roger put much of his energy into racing boats and cars. In July he and his friend Rick Parfitt of Status Quo went to Monaco for the Grand Prix, but missed the race having spent the night in jail after being arrested for being drunk and disorderly. Brian joined up with a group of young musicians and released a mini-album, 'Star Fleet Project'. Freddie lived life to the full in New York, where he now had a spacious, forty-third-floor apartment overlooking Central Park. 'New York is Sin City,' he told the press. 'When I'm here, I can slut myself!' He did spend a little time, however, working on two songs with Michael Jackson at his home studios, and in the days before the younger star became a recluse, the pair even went out clubbing together. The idea was that the songs should appear on Jackson's 'Thriller' album, or on Queen's next album, but the project amounted to nothing and the tapes, half-completed, still lie in a Hollywood vault.

In the summer of 1983, another tour of South America was booked, unwisely in the aftermath of the Falklands War, with six concerts scheduled. Following heated exchanges over finances and politics, this was quickly aborted. By the middle of August, however, they were together again – refreshed and brimming with new ideas, working at the Record Plant Studios in Los Angeles on the score for the film *The Hotel New Hampshire*, based on the novel by John Irving. The film was to be directed by one of Britain's most inspired cinematographers, Tony Richardson, famous for *Saturday Night and Sunday Morning*, *A Taste of Honey* and *Tom Jones*. Married at the time to Vanessa Redgrave, Richardson – who would die of AIDS just before Freddie – certainly showed more than a passing interest in Freddie, but one which was not reciprocated. This may or may not have had something to do with Queen's music not being used for the film, though much of it was put to better use when they decided to incorporate it into their new album, 'The Works', which became the focal project of their ten-week stay at the

Record Plan. Released in February 1984, Queen's thirteenth album would reach Number 2 in the charts. One song, Freddie's portentous, autobiographical *Keep Passing the Open Windows* – a phrase used repeatedly by Irving throughout his book – sadly not as well known as the other tracks on the album, was retained in its entirety.

At around this time, too, Queen changed their American record label. For some time they had been dissatisfied with the way Elektra had been handling their output, so they signed with Capitol. Through Jim Beach, they forked out $1 million for the privilege of terminating their contract – a worthwhile sacrifice, they hoped.

Back in September 1983 one of the guests at Freddie's birthday party in Los Angeles had been the film producer, Giorgio Moroder, probably best known at the time for *Flashdance*. Moroder had recently purchased the rights to Fritz Lang's 1926 silent epic *Metropolis*, with a view to restoring and re-releasing it the following year. The talents of Bonnie Tyler, Pat Benetar and several minor acts had already been commissioned. What Moroder now needed was some appropriately sci-fi music to augment the score and, having marvelled at their work for *Flash Gordon*, he approached Queen. The group made Moroder an offer he could hardly refuse: in exchange for exclusive rights to a few fragments from the film, to do with as they wished, Queen would supply the producer with his music.

Metropolis, German-born Lang's prophecy of the Hitler regime, was a nightmare fantasy of machines, power and drudgery, inspired by the director's first impression of New York. Rulers live in skyscrapers, whereas the dehumanized workers toil underground, never resting in this symbolically controlled city. Anarchy erupts when Freder, the son of the leading industrialist (played by Gustav Fröhlich, who bore an uncanny resemblance to Freddie) falls in love with Maria, one of the workers, resulting in the creation of a robotized Maria who incites her fellows to revolt – an insurrection which goes wrong when Freder supports them and not his father. Thus the city is left in ruins, and the industrialist is compelled to call a truce and swear a dramatic oath of friendship.

Several clips from *Metropolis* were incorporated into the video for the first single to be taken from 'The Works'. Roger Taylor's song had started out life as *Radio Ka Ka*, a title suggested by his small son, who, upon listening to something on the radio that he had disliked, had applied the term he usually used when he wanted to go to the toilet. On Freddie's insistence, this was changed to *Radio Ga Ga*, though the theory behind Taylor's absurd lyrics and engaging melody remained unchanged, as Freddie explained, 'It now seems that videos are more important than radio. But if videos *are* taking over, what is radio going to do? It's the downside of MTV. Every time you hear a song, you automatically picture the video. Of course, the funny thing about *Radio Ga Ga* is that we then had to rush out and *do* a video!'

The single was released at the end of January 1984, and peaked at Number 2 in the charts – prevented from hitting the jackpot by Frankie Goes to Hollywood's definitive gay-sex classic, *Relax*. David Mallet's video, which cost a staggering £110,000 to make, was filmed at Shepperton Studios. Fritz Lang had engaged a cast of 30,000 for his film, but Queen had to make do with a mere 500 extras – fans who were drafted in, dressed in white boiler suits, sprayed with silver paint, and instructed to bow their heads in submission while clapping their hands repeatedly in unison with the group, a task which took twelve hours to complete because *Queen* kept getting it wrong. The four members were then cleverly incorporated into the film's theme, sometimes into the actual sepia footage: riding on the overhead motorway and, in a blackout vignette representing a future holocaust, coming to life in an audacious Queen-only video kaleidoscope when a gas-masked family reach for their *Favourite Years* book. Freddie also took advantage of his resemblance to Gustav Fröhlich by replacing him in the 'Hands of Time' sequence, though by far the most ingenious piece of splicing comes when his face materializes within that of the robot, instead of Maria's. It is safe to say that, of all Queen videos thus far – Bohemian Rhapsody aside, of course – the one for *Radio Ga Ga* was easily the most distinguished.

Hot on the heels of *Radio Ga Ga* was the single, *I Want to Break Free*, and if David Mallet's video for this was only marginally less exciting than his last, it was more expensive to make and certainly proved controversial – though on reflection, one may only wonder why. Its theme centred around the drudgery of a provincial Northern town, and was based upon Britain's longest-running soap-opera, 'Coronation Street'.

Dreary back-to-back terraced houses and an exploding teasmaid open the scenario which features all four members of Queen in drag: Brian May, as Mother, in pink nightdress and hair-curlers; John Deacon, the Grannie who preoccupies herself with the newspaper headline, 'Rock 'n' Roll Earl Weds the Typist'; Roger Taylor, so utterly convincing and gorgeous as the bimbette schoolgirl that many fans refused to believe that it was him; and Freddie, the most outrageous of all – still moustachioed, wearing a pink top, black leather mini-skirt, suspenders and high heels, vacuuming the carpet and prancing up and down with a feather duster until, flinging open the larder door, he enters *à la* 'Stars in Their Eyes' into the world of his dreams. Four hundred miners in black boiler-suits and helmets (Queen fans, once more) escort him underground to the fawn's lair, where he re-creates the celebrated Nijinsky role for the first time on celluloid, with a full *corps de ballet*, posturing, preening and body-swimming across a row of prostrated dancers, until the bubble bursts and he is transported back to working-class reality.

The music press, who over the years had gained a

monopoly on mockery and lampoonery, refused to see the funny side of Queen's 'Carry On'-style humour. One publication branded them 'a bunch of transvestites', another accused them of inciting fans 'towards their own brand of blatant homosexuality'. *I Want to Break Free* was also an exercise in record company greed, at a time when such practices were not as commonplace as they are today. No fewer than six different covers went on sale: four 7-inch singles depicting the individual members of the group, and two 12-inch singles with collective shots. Even so, it reached Number 3 in Britain, and was a phenomenal success around the world – particularly in South America, where in some countries (who as yet had not seen the video) it was adopted as an anthem against political oppression.

In the spring of 1984 Freddie returned to Munich, where he set up court at the Arabella-Haus Hotel, flitting back and forth to the studio to work on his first solo album, a project with which he had been preoccupied for some time. In April he appeared as part of a photo-feature for *Vogue* – about diamonds. A few weeks later he and Queen performed at the Golden Rose Festival, in Switzerland – an event which he loathed because all the artists were expected to mime to their records, and one which he turned into a farce by deliberately miming out of synch. And of course, Freddie's evenings were never short of riotous, almost exclusively turned over to hedonistic pursuit, with Winnie Kirkenberger and Barbara Valentin . . . until the night of 22 May when, very much the worse for wear and wholly out of character, he got himself involved in a brawl and tore the ligaments of his leg, resulting in having to spend three weeks in a toe-to-thigh plaster cast, incapacitated maybe, but still raising merry hell.

Only days after the plaster-cast was removed, Queen filmed the video for their next single, *It's a Hard Life*. This opened with Freddie belting out a few bars from Leoncavallo's 'I Pagliacci', so naturally the setting was a masquerade ball – and while the other members of the group looked distinguished in their brocades and ruffs, Freddie of course quite effortlessly managed to make himself the star of the show. An admirer of the legendary French star Mistinguett – famous for her fabulous legs, temper tantrums, and staircase tableaux at the Casino de Paris – he decided that he would emulate her, and commissioned a stunning one-piece scarlet outfit, cut to display one half of his torso and leaving one foot bare, and decorated with twenty-six large eyes, feathers and a number of costly rare egrets which Mistinguett herself had worn in her 1938 revue, 'Féerie de Paris'.

The single reached Number 6 in the charts, and was followed quickly by yet another track from the album, *Hammer to Fall*, on 10 September. (By the end of the year, every song on the album would have been put out as an A or B side of a single, infuriating the critics and many fans . . . who bought them again all the same.) On the same day the *We Will Rock You* video was released, and Freddie's first solo single, *Love Kills*, from the *Metropolis* soundtrack. Though nowhere near as definitive as his later solo efforts, it was nevertheless a well-received début which soared into the top Ten – something none of the other Queen members had achieved in their individual projects, which must have been very disconcerting for them at the time.

Queen's European tour, their first in more than two years, began in Belgium at that old stalwart, the Forêt Nationale de Bruxelles, on 24 August 1984. From there it progressed triumphantly with dates in Eire, England, France, Italy (their first major concerts in that country) and Germany, until another unlucky 22nd – of September – when Freddie took an onstage tumble at Hanover's Europhalle, injuring the ligaments in his knee and forcing him to complete his act seated at the piano. He was treated at a local hospital, and was advised to take at least a week's rest. Two days later, however, he was wowing fans in Berlin, and the tour continued without further hitch, closing in Vienna on the last day of the month. Queen then embarked on what would remain their most controversial project: twelve scheduled concerts in South Africa, at the Superbowl in Bophuthat-swana's Sun City Complex.

The group's headstrong decision to work in a country torn apart by apartheid caused tremendous consternation among all sections of the media, as well as within the Musicians Union, who strongly advised them not to go. Sun City was a Las Vegas-style millionaires' paradise, part-financed by the South African government, situated smack in the middle of one of the most squalid, poverty-stricken townships in the world. Many great stars of the past had rallied to perform before mixed audiences – not just black entertainers such as Joséphine Baker, Billie Holiday and Lena Horne, but the likes of Marlene Dietrich and Gracie Fields, but with them remuneration had always been secondary to fighting racial prejudice and segregation. Effectively, any artist willing to play Sun City was regarded as insensitive, oblivious towards the suffering of others and just downright greedy. What made this particular trip appear even more avaricious than it probably was, however, were the varying statements given to the press before and after the event – Brian May declaring that Queen had always been completely nonpolitical, while John Deacon refuted this by saying, 'We're totally against apartheid and all it stands for.' Freddie only made matters worse by telling the press, 'There's *such* a lot of money to be made out there, my dear!'

The first show took place amid great tension and stringent security on 5 October, though it was an unexpected disaster which almost brought the proceedings to a halt when, several songs into their set, Freddie began experiencing pain in his throat. He did manage to struggle through till the end of the evening, but when the specialist flown in the next day ordered him to rest his vocal chords completely, or risk never being able to sing again, he backed down and the next four concerts at the 7,000-seater Superbowl were cancelled. Thus, while the other members of the group explored the world of the average Black South African – having learned that the incarcerated Nelson Mandela's African Nationalist Party had unofficially adopted *I Want to Break Free* as its anthem – Freddie submitted to the quiet atmosphere and questionable pleasures of his hotel suite. There was one excursion, to the Kutlawamong School for Blind and Deaf Children, where, completely unbeknown to his entourage, Freddie handed over a huge sum of money – cash which, along with the royalties from an album of one of Queen's concerts, effectively prevented the school from closure.

Upon their return to England, Queen were ostracized by the Musicians Union. Despite an impassioned speech from Brian May to their General Committee under the theme, 'Music should transcend *all* barriers, unfettered by race and politics,' Queen had to pay a hefty fine for breaking the anti-apartheid cultural boycott. Much worse than this, their names were added to a United Nations' blacklist which ostensibly forbade them from ever setting foot in South Africa again while the country was politically unsound.

It was almost a case of 'out of the frying pan and into the fire' in January 1985, when Queen flew to Brazil to perform at the Rock In Rio Festival – a week-long extravaganza promoted as the biggest such event in rock history, featuring a large number of local groups, together with headliners such as Iron Maiden, Def Leppard and James Taylor. 'It was awe-inspiring and mind-boggling to be up there with all those people in the palm of your hand,' Freddie told Sharon Feinstein of the *News of the World*. 'But the other side of the coin is that, though I was surrounded by masses of people who loved me, I must have been the loneliest person there.' Then he added, with crippling sincerity, 'Can you imagine how terrible it is when you've got everything and you're still desperately lonely? *That* is awful beyond words.'

Only recently, of course, Queen had vowed never to visit

South America again. This time, the deciding factor was not the fans or conquering new ground but money and lots of it. The group insisted on raking in even more by demanding the rights to their concert from the local television company who broadcast it live, so that they could release it on video. The first of their two shows took place on 12 January at the Barra da Tijuca, in Rio at 2.00 a.m. in the pouring rain, in front of 250,000 people who sang along and screamed for more all the way through their set until the curtain-call, *I Want to Break Free*. Quite innocuously, Freddie minced on to the stage wearing the wig and upper half of the costume he had worn in the video, which hardly anyone in this part of the world had seen.

First of all, a scuffle broke out when one of the security men started hassling a young man who had emulated Freddie by shoving two oranges down his vest. Then, as if on cue, hundreds of fans standing near the stage began pelting the group with anything that came to hand – bottles, cans, stones and shoes – until Freddie saw the light and removed his top and 'falsies', whereupon they just as quickly settled down. He was later told the reason for their outrage. By performing *his* song in that way, he had offered the supreme insult against *their* anthem against dictatorship.

Unusually, too, the post-gig party – at the Copacana Beach Hotel – was televised live, which may explain the reason why it was a pretty tame affair by Queen's standards. One or two outbreaks of typical behaviour were captured on film, however, including Freddie's bitchy argument with Rod Stewart, who had apparently gatecrashed the party, very quickly become drunk, then refused the summons to Freddie's table.

After Rio, Freddie spent several weeks commuting between London – clubbing and having riotous fun – and Munich, where he completed his first solo album, which he had decided to call 'Mr Bad Guy'. The first single from this, *I Was Born To Love You*, c/w a non-album track, *Stop All*

The Fighting, was released on 8 April, on the eve of Queen's tour of Australasia and Japan, and reached Number 11 in the charts. The video, again by David Mallet, featured hundreds of goose-stepping women wearing red plastic breastplates and high heels, and is said to have been inspired by the busty Barbara Valentin.

Queen's stay in Melbourne, between 16 and 20 April, almost ended in disaster when Freddie was asked to appear on 'Countdown', a popular television pop chat-show hosted by Ian 'Molly' Meldrum. The previous September, when his friend Divine had been about to tour Australia for the first time, Meldrum had called for a ban on the star – not because of his outrageous stage show, but because Meldrum had deemed Divine's films with John Waters, which he had never seen, as pornographic. 'Divi was convicted without so much as a trial,' Freddie had blazed at the time, adding, 'Meldrum is a homophobe, and if ever *I* get the chance to meet him, I'll give him a piece of my mind!'

This never happened, though Freddie certainly embarrassed his host in front of millions of viewers when Meldrum asked him how he had persuaded the other members of Queen to drag up for the video of *I Want to Break Free*, responding, 'They ran for *their* frocks quicker than anything, dear!' The next morning, in some of the tabloids, the group were once again wrongly accused of 'perverting' fans.

By this time there was another regular man in Freddie's life. Jim Hutton was a thirty-five-year-old hard-drinking Irishman who worked as a gentlemen's barber at the Savoy Hotel, a Burt Reynolds clone of whom Freddie told a German reporter, 'Piaf did it, and so did Streisand. Now *I* have a hairdresser husband, dear!'

Freddie and Hutton had met briefly at the end of 1983 at a Kensington gay club. According to Hutton, Freddie – whom he did not even recognize, having never heard of Queen – offered to buy his near-lookalike a drink, only to be told,

'Fuck off!' The pair had since bumped into each other several times, but the ice had not been broken between them until March 1985, when they had danced together at Heaven, one of Freddie's regular London haunts. Again according to Hutton, Freddie's opening line had been, 'How big is your dick?' Needless to say, they had spent the night together, though it would take a while for their relationship to become serious. Meanwhile, Hutton began spending his weekends with Freddie in Munich, where the singer was still seeing Winnie Kirkenberger – not out of mischief, it would appear, but because he did not have the heart to tell him that he had fallen in love with someone else.

Hutton does not appear to have minded being two-timed, but when Kirkenberger learned that there was another man in Freddie's life at least as cherished as he was, in a fit of pique he sold the car which Freddie had given him. For Freddie this was the last straw. Soon afterwards he left Munich, and finally moved into Garden Lodge.

On 29 April 1985 'Mr Bad Guy' was released by CBS. The album was dedicated to Jerry, his recently deceased cat, and once he had acknowledged the other members of Queen 'for not interfering', Freddie insisted in adding to the sleeve notes, 'Special thanks to Mary Austin, Barbara Valentin for big tits, Winnie for board and lodging . . . Screw everybody else!' It reached Number 6 in the charts, surprising his critics from the music press who, unable to define a venture which was as far removed from Freddie's work with Queen as could be imagined, simply chose to defile it, and the unalterable fact that over the next six months, five of its tracks would be repeated on A- or B-sides of singles, all of them comparative flops.

Made In Heaven (July) featured a David Mallet video wherein Freddie danced extracts from Dante's *Inferno*, and Stravinsky's *Le Sacre Du Printemps*, in a specially built replica of London's Royal Opera House. *Living On My Own* c/w *My Love Is Dangerous* (September) had its video banned by CBS before any of Freddie's fans could see it and judge for themselves. It featured footage of Freddie's thirty-ninth birthday party at Henderson's nightclub in Munich, a Truman Capote-style Black-And-White Ball, but with the added dimension of cross-dressing. Freddie had forked out several thousand pounds to transform the club to his satisfaction – on top of the £50,000 for the bash itself. The furnishings were replaced, the toilets and dining-room completely renovated, and the place was decorated from top to bottom with black and white roses. Then, for the final single from the album, *Love Me Like There's No Tomorrow*, c/w *Let's Turn It On*, CBS attempted, but failed, to get the fans to part with their money by giving away copies of the 12-inch version of the previous single with copies of the new one, just before EMI jumped on the bandwagon by issuing 'The Complete Works', a limited edition boxed *intégrale* of twelve of Queen's albums. In the hope of ensuring sales, the bait this time was a complimentary album, 'One Vision', containing seven songs which had never appeared on albums – a privilege which set fans back a cool £70.

Many of Freddie's admirers, but not his close friends, had been surprised to learn from the album dedication that Mary Austin was still the most important person in his life, bearing in mind they were no longer lovers and that their split, according to the tabloids, had been acrimonious. Now it emerged that he had only recently changed his will, bequeathing her almost everything. In a rare in-depth interview with Sharon Feinstein of the *News of the World*, he poured out his feelings for this extraordinarily caring woman.

We look after each other, and that's a wonderful form of love. I might have all the problems in the world, but I have Mary, and that gets me through. What better person to leave my fortune to when I go? Of course, my parents are in my will, and so are my cats, but the vast bulk of it will go to Mary. If I dropped dead tomorrow, Mary's the one person I know who could cope with my vast wealth. She's in charge of all my money and possessions, the chauffeurs, maids, gardeners, accountants and lawyers. All *I* have to do is throw my carcass around on stage.

7

To Fly Beyond the Moon

During the spring of 1985 Jim Beach had been approached by former Boomtown Rats frontman-turned-do-gooder Bob Geldof, and asked if Queen might consider participating in his proposed summer extravaganza 'Live Aid' – all but finalized, with mass concerts at the JFK Stadium in Philadelphia and London's 72,000-capacity Wembley Stadium, to raise money for the starving millions of war-ravaged Ethiopia. 'Tell the old faggot it's going to be the biggest thing that ever whatsit happened,' Geldof told Jim Beach, with an irreverence which would continue over the next few months. That may have been the reason why the group hedged, initially: there was no guarantee that the project would work, and Queen did not wish to become too involved in an enterprise which might make them appear foolish. It was only when Geldof spoke to them personally that they agreed to take part.

The event was finally fixed for 13 July, and each of the

many acts engaged was allotted a twenty-minute slot. This was the cue for a series of extremely bitchy backstage cat-fights. Regardless of the fact that it was for charity, 'Live Aid' would prove an ideal vehicle for some faded stars, way past their sell-by date, to resurrect their flagging careers. Morrissey, the frontman from the Smiths, one of Britain's biggest groups who refused to join the bill on principle, also spoke up for the millions of British people who were against the event: 'If "Live Aid" had been organized to confront problems in *this* country, the event would not have taken place.' Each of the acts, too, for purely selfish reasons, attempted to sweet-talk Harvey Goldsmith, Geldof's promoter, into allowing them to close the show. Only Queen wanted to go on in the middle, a decision which earned them a great deal of respect from even their harshest detractors.

Whereas almost everyone involved with 'Live Aid' either threw their sets together willy-nilly, or plugged their latest records, Queen took the event very seriously and hired the Shaw Theatre near King's Cross station, for three weeks of rehearsals which were as intense and thorough as they would have been for any concert. Only a chance remark by Roger Taylor – 'It'll make a pot of money for a wonderful cause, but make no mistake, we're doing it for our own glory as well!' – could have cast serious doubts on their benevolence. Taylor was right of course, especially as Queen's 'Greatest Hits' and 'The Works' album, along with 'Mr Bad Guy', quickly returned to the charts after 'Live Aid', but hypocritical in launching a vitriolic attack against the DJ, Jonathan King, for stating that Geldof had organized the whole affair as an exercise in self-glorification.

The dividend paid off handsomely, with no expense incurred on fancy lights and costumes. Freddie wore ordinary tight-fitting denims and a simple white athletic vest, and watched by an estimated world audience of two billion, Queen stole the show, demoting everyone else on the bill to the status of also-ran. Elton John, David Bowie and

Madonna, superstars in their own right, were dismissed by the *Independent* as 'buskers in makeshift combos'. In one fell swoop, too, Queen righted the wrongs perpetrated by their visit to South Africa, at least as far as the press were concerned.

Bob Geldof told a press conference, 'Queen were absolutely the best band of the day, whatever your personal preference. They had the best sound, they played best, and it was the perfect stage for Freddie. He could ponce about in front of the whole world.' What he did not add, a fact which was observed by almost every journalist who witnessed the event, was that Freddie Mercury was the heart and soul, the ultimate driving force behind Queen, that it had been his day, and his alone.

'Live Aid' was the first rock concert that Jim Hutton had attended, and he reflected proudly, 'To see Freddie up there controlling that crowd, tears welled up and the hairs on my neck stood on end.'

Immediately after 'Live Aid' Queen were approached by Russell Mulcahy, at that time known only for his promotional pop videos, and asked to contribute to the soundtrack of his first feature film, then well into production. Starring two unquestionable heart-throbs from different generations – Christopher Lambert and Sean Connery – *Highlander* was a swashbuckling fantasy recounting the bloodthirsty adventures of a time-travelling Scottish warrior and his fight for supremacy against other immortals. As usual, the group demanded top billing; they would provide a minimum two songs, but only if Mulcahy used one of them for the title-track. The director in fact compromised by having Queen do the entire soundtrack for the film and, as with *Flash Gordon*, they decided that all the songs would be slightly amended and released on an album. 'A Kind of Magic' would do even better than its soundtrack predecessor, topping the British charts during the summer of 1986 and reaching the Top Ten in some forty other countries. As for *Highlander*, it had a particularly privileged world première – not in a huge cinema, attended by the glitterati of the entertainment world, but in Great Yarmouth at Queen's very first International Fan Club Convention.

The group's choice for their début single from the album, in retrospect, was not a wise one. Although *One Vision* had as its basis Martin Luther King's famous 'I Have A Dream' speech, the media immediately drew parallels with 'Live Aid', and accused Queen of cashing in on a tragic situation – particularly as the idea for the 'One heart, one soul, just one solution' lyrics had come from Roger Taylor, so soon after his admission that one of the group's main reasons for appearing in 'Live Aid' had been for personal glory.

Several publications actually insisted that all the royalties from *One Vision* be donated to 'Live Aid' because the song's press-release declared that it had been inspired by the event. What they seemed to overlook completely was the fact that one of their 'Live Aid' songs, *Is This The World We Created?*, had earned thousands of pounds for the Save The Children Fund. Two other Queen songs had been included on an album for Greenpeace, enabling their names to be engraved on a commemorative obelisk . . . in Antarctica. Neither did the media pay much attention to Freddie's contribution to 'Fashion Aid', which took place at the Royal Albert Hall on 5 November. Freddie wore a braided jacket made by David and Elizabeth Emmanuel, while his escort for the evening, the actress Jane Seymour, wore a resplendent wedding dress not dissimilar to the one the couturiers had made for the Princess of Wales. Freddie was in his element, posing for photographs with Shirley Bassey and sharing a jar with one of his idols, Julie Goodyear, who played barmaid Bet Lynch in 'Coronation Street'.

There were further problems at the end of the year when the artistic director of Bophuthatswana's Sun City Complex, Hazel Feldman, visited London with the intention of recruiting a number of artists, including Queen, for a return visit to South Africa. No one may now be sure if any discussions actually took place with the group, though Feldman did announce to the music press, 'A return appearance by Queen should not be ruled out.' In order to extricate themselves from what might have become an explosive political situation, the group were compelled to issue a formal statement, 'Queen categorically state that they have no plans at present to return to Sun City. They wish to make it plain that they have a total abhorrence of apartheid.' And this time there were no flippant comments from Freddie or Roger Taylor.

Much of Queen's time was currently being spent working on the new album, though all four members of the group were involved in solo projects. Freddie was commissioned to work on the score for a German feature film, *Zazou*, contributing a now elusive duet with an unknown singer-friend named Jo Dare. He reacted to photographs and features appearing in the press concerning his 'new' escort, Barbara Valentin, by telling a journalist, 'Barbara and I have formed a kind of bond which is far stronger than anything I've shared with a lover in the last six years.' Like most people, the reporter was not aware of the fact that the pair had been close for several years, or of Freddie's involvement with Jim Hutton, who had by now moved into Garden Lodge, where he would be cautiously introduced to non-friends as 'Mr Mercury's gardener'.

Several years after Freddie's death, Hutton would upset a lot of people by announcing, 'From then on, we lived together as man and wife for the rest of Freddie's life.' It would, however, prove a sometimes stormy six years, with more than a few tears and many arguments, most of them quite vociferous and, on at least one occasion, physically violent. 'Jim was a sweet guy, but he drank like a fish,' Jackie Gunn said. 'And when drunk, he was an ugly drunk.' Jim Jenkins went further:

Jim was particularly embarrassing at some of the Queen

conventions. He would say all sorts of dirty things in front of little girls, about some of the things he and Freddie had supposedly got up to. Once, my friend Ian Bowman, one of the nicest people I've ever met, tweaked Jim's nipple just for fun. He started screaming, 'Only one person's ever been allowed to do that to me!' and there was almost a fight. He was *very* nasty.

At this time Freddie also loaned his considerable talents to his friend Billy Squier's 'Enough is Enough' album, vocalizing on *Love is the Hero* and collaborating on *Lady With the Tenor Sax*. Much more interesting, however, were the two songs he recorded which had been written by a much closer pal, Dave Clark, the singing drummer from the Sixties pop group, the Dave Clark Five. Clark – who once strangely hailed Freddie as 'The Piaf of the Eighties' – was working on a stage musical, *Time*, for Cliff Richard, but all the songs on the soundtrack album were to be performed by independent artists. Besides cutting the title-song, Freddie donned the proverbial hair-shirt for *In My Defence*, a combination of an overpowering, lush melody and a sadly restricted lyric which was nevertheless, in retrospect, a personal credo. 'In my defence, what is there to say?' he asks, before declaring, 'All the mistakes we've made must be faced today . . .'

The video for *Time* was filmed at the Dominion Theatre in London's Tottenham Court Road, where the show was playing to packed audiences every night, with Cliff Richard in the starring role and featuring a hologram of Sir Laurence Olivier. One afternoon there was an incident when Freddie turned up at a matinée performance with a friend. Remembering his visits to the local cinema during his teens, he decided that he wanted to be 'the girl with the tray' and, not content to do things by halves he borrowed a white smock from an usherette and purchased the entire contents of an ice-cream tray. He then paraded up and down the aisles of the theatre, doling out free tubs and cones. However, to expedite the job as soon as he was recognized, he suddenly started throwing them in all directions. Some members of the audience saw the funny side of this and began throwing them back. Others disapproved, sending the theatre manager their dry-cleaning bills.

When Sir Laurence Olivier heard of Freddie's exploits, he and his actress wife, Joan Plowright, invited him to their home for dinner. The greatest ever British actor later recalled that it had been the most enthralling evening with 'oodles of laughter, ribald jokes, and lots of healthy effing and blinding'.

Queen's next single from their forthcoming album was its title-track, Roger Taylor's *A Kind Of Magic*. Released on 17 March 1986, it reached Number 3 in the charts. The video, directed by Russell Mulcahy, was his way of thanking the group for their splendid work on *Highlander*.

Filmed in the then not in use Playhouse Theatre in London's Charing Cross, the video featured Freddie as a Bruantesque magician who, surrounded by the animated characters of the group from the album cover, transforms the other members of the group from derelicts to musicians, then back again. The American sampler single, *Princes Of The Universe*, chosen by CBS against Queen's wishes, proved a flop despite an appealing video for which Christopher Lambert re-created his *Highlander* role. Even so, the group were truly in seventh heaven. 'A King of Magic', their most innovative album in years, was released on 2 June, and regardless of the usual hammering from the music press went straight to the top of the British charts, quickly following suit in Australasia and throughout much of Europe, but barely scraping into the Top Fifty in the United States, one country which had always been full of surprises where record sales were concerned.

That year's 'Magic Tour', arranged and promoted by Harvey Goldsmith, was the biggest, best and costliest ever. The venues were even more huge, all the concerts triumphs of mind over matter not just for Queen but for the road crews and the lighting technicians, who were responsible for hauling the one-hundred-foot stage back and forth across Europe to a staggering twenty-one different venues, and for erecting and maintaining an increasingly complicated ten-ton lighting rig, an operation which alone took forty hours.

The tour kicked off on 7 June at the Rasunda football stadium in Stockholm – a shaky start marred by the heckling of hundreds of anti-apartheid demonstrators and, in the street outside the venue, a noisy protest march by what the press dubbed 'former admirers who have seen the light'. These attempted to badger genuine fans to boycott the show. Queen's set, too, was more varied than usual. As if due to a premonition, it was not just a plug for the new album but included several old hits which had not been aired for years, along with a nifty rock'n'roll medley. 'We're probably the best live band in the world, and we're going to prove it,' an ever-cocky Roger Taylor boasted to the press, adding to Freddie's earlier disclosure, 'We are the Cecil B. de Mille of rock!' As for Freddie's curtain-calls during this tour, the term 'audacious' seemed grossly inadequate. Wearing what many fans believed was genuine royal apparel – an ermine-lined cloak, jewelled crown, orb and sceptre, all designed by his friend Diana Moseley – Freddie was every inch the King of Queen!

The tour progressed through Holland, France, Belgium, Germany and Switzerland with the elements clearly on Queen's side. Then, on 5 July, they played Slane Castle, on the outskirts of Dublin, where it stayed fine long enough for Freddie to pose for photographs wearing his crown and, in some shots, looking decidedly un-regal with a cigarette dangling from the corner of his mouth. The rain that evening had an adverse effect on the crowd, who barely tolerated the support acts – including Chris Rea – before taking their frustration out of each other halfway through Queen's set. Four days later the group played one of the 'small' venues on their circuit, the 40,000-capacity St James Park in Newcastle, the entire proceeds of which they donated to Princess Anne's Save The Children Fund. Then, on 11–12 July they appeared before an audience of 144,000 at Wembley Stadium, a venue which had sold out within hours and which was filmed and recorded in its entirety.

At Wembley, in spite of more rain – 'I expect they paid the heavens handsomely for the special effects!' quipped one reviewer – the fans had the time of their lives, particularly when halfway through the show four huge, helium-filled dummies of the group were launched from the stage. Three failed to get out of the stadium. Claimed by the crowd, they were burst, ripped to shreds and squabbled over as battle trophies. 'Freddie' turned up the next morning . . . in a back garden in Chelmsford.

No great Queen performances, of course, could have been put to bed without the backstage party. In this instance, it was an £80,000 bash at the sumptuous Roof Gardens, atop Marks and Spencer, in Kensington High Street, where no amount of opulence could prevent Freddie and his friends from having the most outrageous time of their lives until dawn, though for once he played things down by arriving with Mary Austin, much to Jim Hutton's dismay. From that day, according to several of Freddie's closest friends, the man and woman in his life would never see eye to eye.

Queen's guests were escorted to the main party area by bellboys and busty women wearing nothing but body-paint designs executed by the artist Bernd Bauer, flown in especially from Munich for the occasion. Drag queens were everywhere, some so convincing that several very straight men were given nasty shocks in the anteroom which had been set up for 'personal' services. Cocaine too was in ready supply – served on silver platters by naked dwarves. In the ladies' powder-room, the 'attendant' was a young man in chains and a studded leather posing-pouch, which Freddie had purchased from the Zipper store in Camden Town. Most outrageous of all, however, were the nude girls in cages in the club's gardens, and the topless blondes offering hand-relief in the gentlemen's lavatories. Revellers Gary Glitter, Mel Smith, Griff Rhys-Jones and Limahl are said to have lapped up every peccadillo thrown at them, though Cliff Richard is thought to have frowned on such behaviour. On the other hand, everyone adored the main event when, in a hilarious spoof, Queen took to the floor as 'Dicky Heart And The Pacemakers', aided by *Sun* Page Three girl Samantha Fox and Gary Glitter, for an impromptu rock'n'roll jam.

After their concert at Manchester's Maine Road football stadium on 16 July, Queen played Cologne, then Vienna, where Freddie was joined by Mary Austin. From here they travelled to their next venue, the 80,000-seater Budapest Nepstadion, built by Stalin, via the River Danube, on Russian President Mikhail Gorbachev's state hydrofoil.

Queen's Hungarian admirers were especially demanding. Whereas great stars such as Marlene Dietrich, Charles Aznavour and Louis Armstrong had taken considerable cuts in their fees to enable their fans to afford to see them, Queen's phenomenal running costs and alleged unwillingness to submit to such a thing resulted in each ticket for their show costing the equivalent of four weeks' wages. None of Queen's records had ever been released in Hungary. They were imported from Yugoslavia, which had already imported some of them from Britain and America, and prices were often exorbitant. 'They'll *have* be good, all things considering,' warned one newspaper.

Beginning with their official reception at the British Embassy, every step of Queen's visit was captured on celluloid and used to augment their *Live In Budapest* video, a concept which was considerably better filmed and edited than their earlier Rio video.

The group were seen waving to fans from their boat, signing the City Book and sunbathing. John Deacon managed to chat with a shy little English girl, Roger Taylor participated in a go-kart race without a crash helmet, and Freddie and Mary Austin were filmed buying prints and antiques. Much of this work was carried out by the state-owned Mafilm company, using every single television camera in the country, and besides being incorporated into the video, the footage was used for documentaries broadcast to Czechoslovakia, Romania and the Soviet Union. But if there was a general feeling of camaraderie among the local media, who could not have done enough to make the group's stay in Budapest a memorable one, the behaviour of the British press over which of their members should or should not be awarded the most preferential treatment, was quite deplorable. Worst of all were the 'lower denomination' (Freddie's term for the music press) whom he awarded the grandiose-sounding title 'Brygada Bosmec', which some reporters printed on their lapel badges and flaunted with pride, until they learned from the local police that 'bosmec' was Hungarian for 'Fuck off'.

Queen's support act at the Nepstadion was the most unusual they would ever have. Z'zi Labor was a local repertory group of forty female folksingers whose average age was fifty, and who performed in traditional costume. Freddie became pally with two of them, regardless of the language problem, and through an interpreter accepted a dare. He learned the words to *Tavaszi Szél Vizét Araszt*, a popular ditty, and promised to incorporate it into Queen's set, providing Z'zi Labor learned and sang the Rolling Stones' *Honky Tonk Woman*, which they did. The Hungarian song would be sung frequently throughout Queen's visit, though during the actual concert itself Freddie had to rely on reading the words off the palm of his hand. Though very brief, with a poignant accompaniment from Brian May this beautiful piece brought the house down.

Although he joked that he had been unable to go even to the toilet without being trailed by the press, Freddie did manage to evade media attention while sampling the more personal delights of Budapest. There were only three known gay bars in the city, all totally respectable, though on account of the country's homophobia they were accessible only through a discreet telephone call, followed by a password spoken into a back-door intercom.

Queen's concert on 27 July was breathtaking, though slightly restrained because their Hungarian fans were not allowed to respond quite as enthusiastically as Western audiences. The police in charge of security there carried sub-machine guns, and a sizeable portion of the audience comprised the green-uniformed Young Guard, a youth organization who were not specifically concerned with who was on the stage, but with the fact that this was the very first rock concert to have been staged in the Eastern bloc. They had been particularly impressed by the statement issued earlier by Gheorghiu Lakos, the local promoter: 'This is the new urban folk music. There is no clash between rock and socialism, here. It is the culture of workers and students, and will improve the image of our country.'

On the positive side, among those closest to the stage were eight hundred genuine fans who had risked the journey into Budapest from two towns across the Ukrainian border, and it was they who whooped and cheered the most, though apparently not enough. 'Even Freddie's posturing has lost any sense of camp or ribaldry,' reported John Gill of *Time Out*. 'The mike-as-penis-extension routine is as clean as "The Jimmy Savile Show", and you could show the bump 'n' grind passages to your gran.'

After Budapest there should have been just four concerts left in Queen's schedule: one in Fréjus in the South of France, and others in Barcelona, Madrid and Marbella. Harvey Goldsmith, however, well aware that he was probably on to the biggest moneyspinner of his career – thus far, the tour had grossed at least £10 million – added a last-minute concert at Knebworth Park, a country house near Stevenage, for 9 August, an event which would give them their largest ever British audience. According to the police reports, which claimed that the event had been oversubscribed, an incredible 193,000 fans flocked to the grounds, creating what was claimed at the time to be the worst ever British traffic-jam. For the fans, of course, it was worth every hassle, and there was plenty to do before the group took to the stage as Goldsmith had provided beer-tents, a dance-hall and even a funfair.

In fact, Queen stole the limelight without playing so much as a single note – while one of the warm-ups, Big Country, were halfway through their set, the group flew overhead in their custom-painted 'Kind of Magic' helicopter, causing utter pandemonium. One young woman went into labour and had her baby in the field, and, more seriously, another fan became involved in a brawl and was stabbed, bleeding to death before help arrived.

Knebworth Park had been an exhausting but inspired event for everyone on both sides of Queen's showbusiness fence, though the press agreed unanimously that, more than ever, Queen was by now more or less a one-man outfit. Andy Stout wrote in *Sounds*:

> Queen are a seriously good live act. Freddie Mercury is perhaps one of the best singers and frontmen rock has ever had. A complete camp ham, yes, but a damn good one. The rest of the group may be musically great and groovy, but they're also sodding boring.

Before leaving the stage, Freddie had told the audience, 'Thank you, you beautiful people. Goodnight, sweet dreams. We love you!' In effect, he was sealing Queen's swansong as a live act, for what no one in that crowd knew then was that they were seeing their beloved idols for the very last time.

8

And Shake the Foundations from the Skies!

For Queen the remaining months of 1986 passed quietly, though not uneventfully. Brian May and John Deacon, committed to respective solo projects, vied for tabloid headlines with exposés on their private lives – May becoming involved with 'Eastenders' star Anita Dobson, Deacon reported to be recovering from what appears to have been a nervous breakdown caused by overwork. Freddie devoted much of his time to the ongoing restorations at Garden Lodge, taking an active interest in the landscaping of his garden and the construction of the large pond which would soon house his collection of beloved Koi carp – taking a break only to organize his birthday party.

This particular birthday – Freddie's fortieth – was fêted with a Mad Hat Party, and was tamer than most of the others. Now that he had revised his sexual proclivities there

126

were no known drugs, no freak entertainers and nudes, just honest-to-goodness fun with two hundred friends. Joe Fanelli, in charge of the catering, wore a creation decorated with dozens of Belgian chocolates, and Mary Austin turned up in a sword-pierced matador's hat. Most important of all, however, was Jim Hutton's surprise – a plain gold wedding-band which Mary Austin is said to have approved, and which for obvious reasons was never worn in public, though it does turn up in several private photographs.

After the party Freddie and Hutton honeymooned in Japan – a twenty-one-day, £1 million shopping spree during which Freddie's purchases were so extensive that most of them had to be taken straight from the stores to a warehouse, where they were crated and shipped to England. And naturally, there was the obligatory trip to the Ginza, where Freddie visited several tea-houses and renewed his acquaintance with Miwa, at his famous club. As a belated birthday present, Miwa performed *Non, Je Ne Regrette Rien* and *Tu Ne Sais Pas Aimer* – the latter a Damia *chanson* which would be used in France as the theme-song for AIDS awareness.

The following afternoon there was a very subdued joint birthday party for Freddie and his Japanese hostess–personal assistant, Misa Watanabe, at her home. This pleased him no end, though Watanabe's surprise for that evening did not go down well at all: she had arranged for him to be guest of honour at the première of an all-Japanese production of Andrew Lloyd Webber's *Cats*, and to attend the backstage party, a hysterical affair which saw him constantly mobbed by members of the cast. He was further angered a few days later when visiting a museum in Chiba, famed for its collection of exquisite blue-and-white 'Hizen' porcelain plates. Freddie tried his utmost to persuade the curator to sell him some of these, but to no avail. All he ended up with was a copy of the catalogue, and a red face.

The couple's flight home to London, diverted to Alaska

because of industrial action, then to Munich on account of adverse weather conditions, was an arduous twenty-four-hour ordeal, and neither man was prepared for the sudden rush of reporters which greeted them at Heathrow. The news of Freddie's recent (allegedly his first) HIV test had been leaked to the press and George Kozikowski, of Harley Street's Jean Shanks Clinic, had apparently disregarded the hippocratic oath by telling the *News of the World*, 'I didn't know he was here until his name unfortunately appeared on a form.'

The newspaper published an exclusive: QUEEN STAR FREDDIE IN AIDS SHOCK, though the editorial did add that the test had proved negative, and that Freddie and Mary Austin were still living as a couple at Garden Lodge. Feeling betrayed, Freddie reacted as one would expect, snarling at the reporters who brandished copies of the *News of the World* feature, and at photographers who tried to snap him at close range for any tell-tale signs, 'Do I *look* like I'm dying of fucking AIDS? I haven't got any sexual disease. Leave me alone!'

In truth, he looked remarkably well, despite the long flight, but his outburst, minus the expletive, appeared as a headline in the *Sun* on 14 November, together with his statement, 'I'm perfectly fit and healthy, thank you. I don't know what anybody has said, but it's all so silly. Of course I'm concerned about my health. Isn't everybody?'

Even so, such media speculation terrified him, compelling him to tone down his lifestyle and be constantly on his guard. Henceforth there would be fewer wild parties, absolutely no one-night stands, and a good many evenings spent at home in front of the television. 'I've stopped going out,' he said. 'I've almost become a nun. I was extremely promiscuous but I've stopped all that. What's more, I don't miss that kind of life.' David Evans, a frequent visitor to Garden Lodge, told me, 'Privately, Freddie would talk about anything but his work – his paintings, shows he had seen, places he'd been to, stars he'd met, how awful Sarah Ferguson looked in her wedding dress. All the camp things that gay boys talk about, but *never* his work.'

The elegant dinner parties – always far removed from Queen's noisy, irreverent shindigs – continued. Mike Moran explained:

> Freddie may have been a very famous guy, but he only had a small circle of friends, and he led a *very* private life. The same people were there all the time: Mary, my wife Linda and myself, Peter Straker and Dave Clark, Freddie's doctor Gordon Atkinson and his boyfriend, Jim and Claudia Beach. The others from the band didn't visit often, except Brian with Anita Dobson. Then occasionally there would be Tim Rice and Elaine Paige, or Barbara Valentin.

A few days after returning from Japan, Freddie received another shock when John Murphy arrived for a holiday in London. Although they were no longer amorously interested in each other, Freddie and he were still very good friends, and each time he visited Los Angeles Freddie would dine with Murphy and his partner, James Wynethorpe. Now, Murphy dropped the bombshell that they were both dying of AIDS. There was, however, worse to come, for no sooner had Murphy settled in at Garden Lodge than he was summoned home – Wynethorpe's health had suddenly deteriorated.

In fact, it was John Murphy who died first, on 11 November 1986, followed a few weeks later by his lover. Freddie was devastated, yet no sooner had this dreadful news sunk in than he received a telephone call from Brighton. Tony Bastin had also died of the disease. Freddie told the press, 'So many of my friends are dying of AIDS. Others won't last much longer, and I'm terrified that I'll be next. I know it's silly, but each time I've made love I jump into the shower and scrub myself clean. Not that it's going to make any difference – I mean, if I've got it already, what can I do?'

In spite of these tragedies, of course, work had to go on and the next few years would find Freddie at his peak, vocally and artistically. At the beginning of 1987 while 'Live Magic' – an edited compilation of highlights from Queen's most recent tour – was riding high in the charts, Freddie began a hugely successful working partnership with Mike Moran, the producer of his 'Time' songs, first at Moran's home studio, then at London's Townhouse Studios, where he recorded Buck Ram's *The Great Pretender*, a huge hit in 1956 for the British star Anne Shelton, and for the American group The Platters, who ironically perhaps had recorded it on the Mercury label. Released on 23 February, it is perhaps the best-loved and most widely known of all Freddie's solo songs, and peaked at Number 4 in the charts. The video, too, was his most stylish since *It's A Hard Life*, and featured yet another staircase descent, together with four hundred Freddie cut-outs, and cameo appearances by Roger Taylor and Peter Straker, wearing drag.

Coinciding with the release of *The Great Pretender*, Freddie granted an interview with one of the few journalists he trusted, David Wigg of the *Daily Express*, who over the past year or so had witnessed several of the singer's tantrums. One when, after his microphone had cut out in the middle of a song, he had stormed into his dressing-room to hurl a steam-iron through a full-length mirror; another at Garden Lodge, when in a fit of pique he had thrown a valuable antique Japanese vase through the window before collapsing on his bed in a flood of tears. Now the conversation was quite perturbing. Not only had he lost John Murphy and Tony Bastin, another friend was dying of AIDS – Kenny Everett's lover Nicolai Grishanovitch, whom Freddie had nicknamed 'The Madam From Minsk', would succumb to the disease the following year. Admitting that he had just tested negative for HIV, Freddie said:

AIDS *has* changed my life. I'm not as promiscuous as I used to be. I've adopted an intelligent approach towards sex – after all, I've had lots of lovers, male *and* female, though all of them have gone wrong. I think *anyone* who has been promiscuous should have a test. You can still have *fun* – you can't expect people to just give up sex, but I think the message people are trying to get over, this thing about safe sex, *is* worthwhile.

But, had he found that crock of gold at the rainbow's end, that special person to share the rest of his life with and, more importantly, if the right person came along, would he be willing to make the ultimate sacrifice? Some months before he had confessed that only two creatures had ever returned the love he had given them: Mary Austin and Jerry, his cat. Now he told David Wigg:

Money can't buy you love, and the more money one makes, the more miserable one becomes. Money attracts all kinds of wrong people. I would not sacrifice my career if a partner wanted me to. It's my career that keeps me going. What else would I do? Dig weeds, get fat and be beautifully in love? No, I'd like to remain as successful as I am, write beautiful songs *and* be in love – not that it's worked up till now, though I'll keep on trying. I've cried rivers. I may be hard on the exterior, but I'm very soft-centered. I'm also a very possessive person. I can go to great lengths, trying to be loyal just to prove a point, but the moment I find someone has betrayed me, I go the other way. Betrayed, I'm an ogre!

Freddie's next project astounded both his fans and friends, and left the critics wondering if he had finally gone mad. His almost manic passion for opera had begun many years before, in Panchgani when as a teenager he had stupified his school chums by listening to the pre-war recordings of Clara

Butt and the great bel canto coloraturas, Amelita Galli-Curci and Elvira di Hidalgo. The latter, during her stay at the Athens Conservatoire during the last war, had been instrumental in launching Maria Callas's career and, in July 1965, Freddie had been talked into seeing Callas's *Tosca* with Tito Gobbi at London's Covent Garden – a friend of his father's had bought two tickets for himself and his girlfriend, and she had been unable to go. It was Callas's last performance on the stage of an actual opera house, and though he later said that he had found the evening overbearing and would not attend another opera for many years, Freddie retained a fondness for the aria, 'Vissi d'arte' – Callas's most requested piece – and once surprised his friend Montserrat Caballé by singing it all the way through, without making one mistake.

At the end of the Seventies, Freddie had developed a passion for the enigmatic German tenor, Fritz Wunderlich, who had died in Munich in 1966 following a fall, aged just thirty-five. Freddie had even visited Wunderlich's hunting-lodge and grave, just outside the city. In 1962, the tenor had sung the role of Tamino in Mozart's *The Magic Flute* for Radio Suisse Romand, in Lausanne, and singing opposite him had been a young Spanish soprano named Montserrat Caballé. Although this recording of his two greatest idols had never been released commercially, in 1980 Freddie had commissioned a copy of the tape from the Swiss radio station – it is to be released in 1997 – and, whilst raving over Wunderlich's magnificent voice, he had been no less impressed by a woman who, by the time he got to know her, was hailed throughout the world as 'La Superba'.

Montserrat herself told me about her first meeting with Freddie Mercury:

It happened in New York, when I was there with Zubin Mehta, the conductor, singing Italian arias from Wagner. Freddie loved Wagner, so he came to the concert and asked to see me. He said, 'Hello, dear. I'm the singer from the group Queen. I'm a huge fan of your "Norma", but I could never imagine you singing Wagner, so I had to hear for myself. I loved it!' Then he explained that he had heard me for the first time in Los Angeles, since which time he had come to several of my performances at the Royal Opera House in London, including my *Tosca* and *Trovatore*. I was very flattered. He knew absolutely everything there was to know about opera. He adored 'Liebestod' from Wagner's *Tristan and Isolde*, and knew all the words. And you should have seen all the videos he had at home – videos of me that I had never even seen myself! He was amazing!

Thirteen years Freddie's senior and from a poor family, Montserrat Caballé had worked in a handkerchief factory in her native Barcelona before being sponsored for a place in the Liceo Conservatoire. Her lucky break had occurred in 1965 when she had stood in for the indisposed Marilyn Horne in a performance of Donizetti's *Lucretia Borgia* at Carnegie Hall, since when she has sung to packed houses all over the world. Then, a few years later she had almost died of cervical cancer and, shortly after her meeting with Freddie, there had been another trauma when, thinking herself to be suffering from no more than a bad dose of flu, she had checked into a New York hospital, only to be diagnosed as having a brain tumour, then refusing surgery when informed by her doctor that it was benign.

In August 1986, during Queen's visit to Barcelona, Freddie had submitted to a rare television interview on the top-rated arts magazine, *Informe Semanal*, and the presenter had asked him if he was interested in Spanish music and, if so, what type. Without hesitation he had declared himself a great Caballé devotee, and he had gone on to praise her formidable courage in the face of adversity.

At the time of Freddie's interview, Montserrat was

touring, but his comments were relayed to her by her brother Carlos, who was also her manager. Montserrat herself told me what had happened next:

> I was in Lausanne when I received a telephone call from the Mayor of Barcelona, asking me if I would sing something for the 1992 Olympics – something aimed at the young people, as a means of attracting them to the city. 'Please don't sing any opera, this time,' he told me, 'Sing something modern!' So I spoke to my brother, and Carlos said, 'Why don't we call Freddie Mercury? He's bound to have an idea what to do!' I agreed, Carlos approached him, and Freddie was so excited. He rented a suite at the Ritz Hotel in Barcelona, and we met him there in December 1986 when I returned from my tour. And you know, as soon as I entered that room I knew I was in the presence of a genius. He came *so* well prepared. So, we discussed our plans, he told me exactly what we would be doing, and we arranged an official business meeting so that the producer, Mike Moran, could be involved.

This meeting – the third between Freddie and his new friend and not the first, as has been often stated – took place over lunch in the same hotel on 27 March 1987. With Montserrat were Carlos Caballé and several members of her entourage, and with Freddie were Peter Freestone and Mike Moran, who told me:

> Freddie and I wrote *Exercises in Free Love* in my studio one night when we were both pissed. We'd done *The Great Pretender*, but we didn't have a B-side. So Freddie said, 'Oh, bugger it, just play something at the piano and we'll see what comes up!' It was three o'clock in the morning and – this is the absolute truth – he said, 'I'll pretend I'm a soprano like Montserrat Caballé!' Then

he started warbling in this falsetto style, and we got the framework of a song, which didn't sound bad. So, we decided to finish it off the next day when we were a bit more *compos mentis*. And now, at the Ritz in Barcelona, Freddie told her, 'I hope you're not offended by this, but this is me, pretending to be you. It's a bit of fun!' We played it, and she listened very carefully. Then she exclaimed, 'Is this for me? It's beautiful. I would really like to perform it – it will be given its world première next week at Covent Garden!' Then she turned to me and said, 'And *you'll* play the piano!'

Over the next few days both Freddie and Mike Moran virtually lived on their nerves, wondering what would happen when one of the world's greatest divas performed their song as her curtain-call for the *crème de la crème* of the social set. In fact, they had absolutely nothing to worry about. *Exercises in Free Love* received a standing ovation.

Afterwards, at Garden Lodge, Freddie and his new partner installed themselves at his grand piano for an impromptu recital of opera, jazz and gospel, which continued until dawn – by which time Montserrat had asked Freddie to compose her a piece about her native city and Catalan heritage. The diva herself suggested several titles, most of them unpronounceable, but it was Freddie who proffered the simplest remedy: 'We'll have to call it Barcelona, dear!'

Montserrat Caballé, of course, was regarded by her devotees and the classical music world as considerably more professional within her art and in her approach than any rock star could ever be. This proved Freddie's greatest challenge. Whereas he and his contemporaries often spent weeks in the studio perfecting and putting together a single track, artists of her calibre simply breezed in between concerts and more often than not completed the recording in one take. According to Mike Moran, however, there was the other side of the coin to be considered:

To be fair, all that opera stars do is to read the printed page, which doesn't deviate that much. If you have a piece of Puccini, you can't change it and to be honest, if you've sung it ten times, you should be able to sing it again. With rock singers, it's more instantly creative – they have the ability and the licence to change it. Freddie and I did all the work, composing and recording her part, which I wrote out for her. All she had to do was come in and sing it. But she loved working with Freddie, of course, because it gave her the opportunity to get away from the stuffiness of the opera world. And she was a *very* funny lady with such a great sense of humour.

The biggest problem facing the Mercury–Caballé partnership was that of availability. When she began working with Freddie in the April of 1987, Montserrat was heavily booked for another three years, which meant that Freddie had to amend his schedule to accommodate what few spare dates she had. 'He was so very, very patient with me,' she said. 'I appreciated that.'

The fact that Montserrat had approached Freddie in the first place to propose this partnership, and not vice-versa, of course says a great deal for the enormous regard he had attracted from outside his own musical sphere – absolutely *no* other rock or pop-star would even have been considered worthy of working with an operatic diva, firstly because he would not be expected to keep up with her, but largely because at that time the concept of combining two such contrasting musical disciplines would have been declared tantamount to blasphemy by the opera world, and ridiculed by rock enthusiasts. For Freddie, however, the consummate professional who had already successfully dipped his toe into classical waters, a new era was about to begin, one which would enable his career to reach unprecedented heights and touch the hearts of an uncharted public. Were it not for the devastating news that he was about to receive, this new facet of his art would almost certainly have seen him working less and less with Queen, though Mike Moran is of the firm opinion that, even approaching middle age, Freddie would never have left the group entirely. 'Cliff Richard and Tina Turner, for instance, are doing stuff today as well as they ever did,' Moran said, adding, 'Freddie may have slightly *modified* his act, perhaps, but he would never have given up his work with Queen because this is what had made him.'

Montserrat Caballé told me what it was like working with Freddie in the studio:

He asked me what I thought of his voice, admitting that when young he had wanted to sing opera. His voice really was that of a baritone, though his fans would of course not have accepted that sort of a voice. So, to prove a point, I got him to sing a duet with me – Violetta's and Germont's 'Dite alla giovine' from *La Traviata*, which I think was taped. He sang it very well. I don't know how much more opera he would have been able to do, though he was such a creative person. I'm sure he would have been able to improvise *anything*. The album itself was very well done. He and Mike Moran made such a good marriage between opera and rock, and it was very well produced. Freddie was a great practical joker – we both liked a laugh, though when we were working it was very serious. And although we were sometimes working for hours at a time, we were never tired or bored. He would come into the studio and say, 'Look, my dear, I have another creation!' Then he would play *La Japonaise*, *Guide Me Home*, or *The Fallen Priest*, the most operatic piece on the album. Working with him was such an inspiration. I had so much respect for his workmanship.

Meanwhile, Freddie's private life took yet another savage

and unexpected battering from the tabloids, and this time it was one of his closest, hitherto most trusted friends who had effectively sold him down the river.

On 4 May 1987 almost the entire front page of the *Sun* was taken up with the headline, 'AIDS KILLS FREDDIE'S 2 LOVERS', beneath which were two photographs: one of Freddie hugging Tony Bastin, the other of he and John Murphy camping it up in women's hats. Inside the newspaper were further headlines: 'POP IDOL'S NIGHT-MARE AS HIS GAY ORGIES RETURN TO HAUNT HIM' and '4 a.m. PHONE CALL OF TERROR'. Paul Prenter had lifted the lid completely off Freddie's private world. On 29 April, we now know, Freddie had called his personal manager in the middle of the night and expressed his fears about dying of AIDS and, after some deliberation, Prenter had contacted a journalist friend and announced that he had a story that was 'white hot'. He had decided to reveal all about Freddie's affairs with Bastin, Murphy and 'hundreds of homosexuals'. Stating that in all his nine years as the singer's right-hand man he had never once seen or heard of Freddie having a relationship with a woman, he added, 'It was more likely that I would see him walk on water than go with a woman.'

Over the next few days, more revelations poured forth. At the end of the Seventies Freddie had assured James Johnson of the *Evening Standard*, 'We're probably the straightest band around. For instance, we were always anti-drugs from the start. We went through all that in our teens, and we never felt that good music comes from being high.' Now, Prenter spoke of Freddie's alleged cocaine binges with David Bowie and Rod Stewart, and of how he and Brian May had often sneaked into the wings during Queen's concerts to snort the drug, of how his one and only musical collaboration with Michael Jackson had been aborted when Jackson had caught him out in his studio, and of how Freddie and Kenny Everett had abruptly ended their friendship after a violent quarrel.

'Kenny had a great capacity for cocaine, but not for paying for it,' Prenter said. 'He accused Freddie of taking all his coke, but it was actually the other way round.'

Worst of all, perhaps, was the grossly misleading picture-spread which appeared in the *Sun* on 7 May, headlined, 'ALL THE QUEEN'S MEN'. 'Freddie Mercury likes men who look as if they can eat a lorry for breakfast,' proclaimed the editorial. Prenter, now described as the singer's *former* personal manager, had opened his private photograph album.

Freddie was depicted stripped to the waist with 'bristly' Big Vince, the perfect American who had refused to relocate to England, with 'snuggly' Winnie Kirkenberger and 'campy' Peter Straker, with 'matey' John Reid and, more suitably attired, with 'zany' Michael Jackson and 'cokey' Rod Stewart. For good measure the newspaper threw in a shot of the man Freddie had always wanted but never even got around to meeting – Burt Reynolds. Confessing how Freddie always went weak at the knees every time he saw the actor's photograph, Prenter added, 'Freddie liked his men big, muscular and rugged, with short hair and a moustache. Burt Reynolds fitted the bill perfectly. Freddie thought he was wonderful, gorgeous. If Burt had walked into the room, I'm sure Freddie would have fainted.'

Freddie hit the roof. 'Paul Prenter wasn't a *horrible* person,' David Evans emphasized. 'He was an easy-going, simple Irish guy. He worked hard and he was passionate about the recording business. He was part of the circus, and when those wheels get rolling they often roll people under them.' Now, not only did Prenter lose an extremely well-paid job, he lost Freddie's friendship and the respect of almost every one of his friends. Freddie also amended his will; had Prenter remained loyal and kept his mouth shut, he would soon have become a wealthy man. Several times over the next few years he would attempt to worm his way back into Freddie's affections, claiming that Richard Ellis of the *Sun* had hounded him into selling him his story, but always to no avail. Not that Freddie had heard the last of Prenter, by any means.

In order to cope with the burden of his problems and troubled state of mind, Freddie hurled himself back into his latest project. His work with Montserrat Caballé was extremely demanding. Because of her bulging diary of commitments, her vocal sections for the album were recorded on tape by Freddie, singing in a curious *mélange* of counter-tenor and coloratura – something he did inordinately well – then forwarded to wherever she was appearing. Their first completed song was *Barcelona*, quickly followed by Freddie's and Mike Moran's *The Fallen Priest*, which they had written in collaboration with Tim Rice. The first time Rice listened to these and their companion masterpiece, *The Golden Boy* in their finished, polished versions, he could only rue the fact that Freddie had never had an opera composed for him. 'Puccini rather than Wagner,' he lamented. 'Freddie was way, way ahead of his time where opera was concerned.' Montserrat Caballé told the press at the time, 'As an opera singer, my voice is an instrument in the hands of the composer. Working with Freddie, my *special* composer, my voice feels free for the first time!'

The pair had great fun working together, the more they got to know each other. Montserrat had a wacky sense of humour and was not stuck up as many opera stars are reputed to be. She loved listening to Freddie's ribald jokes, and was never offended by his colourful language. According to Jim Hutton, the first words she spoke in Garden Lodge – after she had tripped over a loose carpet – were, 'Oh, shit!'

David Evans also recounted an amusing anecdote concerning one of Montserrat Caballé's more unusual gifts to her friend:

Montsy didn't quite know what to send Freddie as a thank you present for working with her. Then one day one of her operatic costumes arrived in the post. I think

it was the one she'd worn some years before when she'd
played Juliet. And what do you do with a dress? You
have to display it! So Freddie put it on some sort of form
to fill it out, and it was placed inside a glass case and
hung halfway up one of the huge piers in his
drawing-room so that everybody could see it. It
certainly was a conversation piece!

Barcelona, the pair's most celebrated and challenging
rock-opera-symphonic *chef-d'oeuvre*, was premièred on 30
May before an invited audience of 6,000 at the Ku Club, an
infamous society night spot in San Antonio, on the island of
Ibiza. The extravaganza was to promote 'Expo 92', the
500th anniversary of the discovery of America, and most
importantly Barcelona's hosting of the 1992 Olympics, for
which the song was to be the official anthem. There were also
contributions from many international stars, including
Duran Duran, Harrison Ford, Maradona, Chris Rea, Roman
Polanski and Spandau Ballet, and it was televised throughout
most of the world. South Africa was one of the few
exceptions, though the plight of that country was referred to
when a singer named Nona Hendrix dedicated a song, *Winds
of Change*, to Nelson Mandela, before diving into the pool
and hitting her head on the bottom, which earned her several
stitches and a waspish comment from Freddie, 'It's a pity
they didn't stitch up her mouth *before* she sang!'

Closing the evening before a scintillating backdrop of
multicoloured fountains and fireworks – one which was
partially re-created in David Mallett's excellent video, aided
by some 300 fans holding disposable cigarette lighters –
Freddie wore a fetching blue dress-suit and cummerbund,
and Montserrat a sparkling, voluminous gown for what Tim
de Lisle described as, 'An exercise in high camp, with two of
the world's most distinguished practitioners vying to see who
could go furthest over the top.' The standing ovation after
Barcelona, not surprising considering the location, lasted

almost as long as the song. Freddie told the coterie of press –
probably unaware that most of them were obviously blind to
their talent and only interested in lampooning the pair for
Freddie's arch-campness and Montserrat's size – 'I defy any
other rock 'n' roll personality living to duet with a legendary
opera diva, and survive!' This flamboyant statement only
provoked the media into penning a series of so-called reviews
which, besides being entirely dismissive of one of the finest
pieces either star had ever recorded, were virulently
offensive. Both Freddie and Montserrat seriously considered
suing *Melody Maker* and the *NME* – but decided not to
when they realized that the adverse publicity was working in
their favour. The single, released at the end of October 1987,
reached Number 8 in the British charts, and made the Top
Ten all over Europe. In Spain, a country which did not
favour singles, the entire 20,000 pressing sold out in just
three hours!

Ibiza was also the setting for Freddie's forty-first birthday
party in September. Of the 400 or so guests, eighty of his
closest friends were flown in from Heathrow on a chartered
DC9, then transported in a fleet of taxis to Pykes, one of the
island's most exclusive hotels, where the Olympic Committee had organized and paid for a sumptuous bash with
flamenco dancers, a fireworks display spelling Freddie's
name in huge letters, and a ten-foot cake decorated with the
opening lines of *Barcelona*. Freddie was despondent when he
learned that Montserrat Caballé could not be there because
she was giving a recital in Stockholm, though she did sing
'Happy Birthday' down the telephone.

Freddie's continuing involvement with Montserrat
Caballé, along with the rest of the group's extra-curricular
activities, fuelled yet more rumours that Queen were about
to split. Roger Taylor had already formed his own group,
The Cross, with himself as vocalist. 'Of course Queen
haven't split up,' he reacted angrily in *Kerrang!* 'But the band
has had a good run over the last couple of years, and we all

decided that we would shut up for a couple of years and give people a rest, especially the brainless idiots of Radio One who are probably sick of having to play Queen singles for the past fifteen years, or whatever!'

Freddie, on the other hand, liked to look upon these solo projects as a survival test, and said in a radio interview:

> We could all just go away and say we've had enough and live happily ever after, but I don't think that's what we're in. We're in it to make music, and what else can I do? This is the thing that interests me most. You don't know what it means when you write a song that people actually appreciate and they *say* it's a good song. It's a *wonderful* feeling! We've all had ego problems, but we've never let it go that far where we've actually said forget it, because the four of us have this chemistry that's worked so well for us. So why kill the goose that lays the golden egg? We will just carry on until one of us drops dead, or something, or is just replaced. I think if I suddenly left, they'd have the mechanism to replace me. Not easy to replace me, hah!

The Cross released numerous singles and three albums, none of which sold well, though one of their songs, *Heaven For Everyone* with Freddie on vocals, was revived with tremendous success by Queen some years later. It is said, however, that Freddie only worked with the ensemble out of loyalty to Roger Taylor, and that he disliked the other members of The Cross. Jim Hutton would later remember their rowdy, slobbish behaviour at one of Freddie's birthday parties, and his comment, 'What a pain they were. They're never coming here again.'

Brian May's projects, for the time being, were even less commendable. Anita Dobson had had a huge hit in 1986 with May's production of *Anyone Can Fall In Love*, the theme from 'EastEnders' which was little more than a novelty number. The critics were unanimous in stating that she was a far better actress than she would ever be a singer, and forecast great things when she signed to star opposite Adam Faith in the stage-musical version of his television hit-series, 'Budgie'. Her other work with Brian May was unbelievably dire, though there was much worse to come when one of the finest rock musicians of all time teamed up with the spoof group Bad News – an outfit comprising the alternative comedians Ade Edmondson, Peter Richardson, Rick Mayall and Nigel Planer from television's 'The Comic Strip'. 'Get Your Hands Round A 12-Inch Now!' screamed the publicity posters for their début album. 'Brian was head-over-heels in love with Anita, and he allowed this to cloud his professional judgement,' a Queen spokesman told me. 'And Bad News's rendition of *Bohemian Rhapsody*, with John and Roger caterwauling all the "Gallileos", was nothing short of sacrilege. Freddie *pretended* to accept what they'd done, but in reality he was furious and wanted to punch Brian's lights out.'

When told that there was no evading the fact that, from a commercial angle and owing to a lack of public performances, Queen's popularity appeared to be on the wane – ever more so in the United States, where some radio stations were no longer playing their records – Freddie told his favourite journalist, David Wigg of the *Daily Express*, 'There are no plans to take on a grand tour at the moment, but we *are* still working together. Just wait and see!'

The fans were placated, to a certain extent, by the release of three videos. *Queen – The Magic Years* was directed by Rudi Dolezal and Hannes Rossacher, 'The Torpedo Twins', and documented the story so far with rare concert footage, glimpses of the group working, laughing and cursing in the studio, and a wealth of anecdotes from friends and colleagues. Small sections of the films were, however, downright annoying and gratuitous, such as the nonsensical comments from the likes of racing-driver Jackie Stewart,

Status Quo and a handful of comparatively unimportant pop stars who giggled and fidgeted and did not seem to know why they were being filmed. Elton John also made several cameo appearances, irksomely referring to Freddie as 'she'.

It is now known that Freddie had held back during his in-depth interview with David Wigg over his HIV test – the fact that only days before speaking to the journalist the results of this and a subsequent test had confirmed the worst. Not only was Freddie most definitely HIV positive, he quite likely had already developed full-blown AIDS. Wigg must therefore be excused for posing a question which had been asked many times, long before there had been any rumours of Freddie being unwell: What would happen to his vast antiques collection after his death? Freddie must really have put on a brave face to respond jokingly, 'I want to be *buried* with all my treasures, like the Pharaohs. If I can afford it, I'll have a pyramid built in Kensington. Now wouldn't *that* be fab?'

David Wigg and many others who were reasonably close to Freddie, though not close enough to know all the details, did of course have their suspicions concerning his health. 'It was very difficult for me,' Wigg confessed. 'I feared something may have been wrong when I met him at his birthday party in Ibiza, but couldn't be sure because he was in such a good mood.'

The first person Freddie confided in about his illness was his great friend, Montserrat Caballé, who choked back the tears as she told me:

Freddie was not a coward, and he was not afraid of facing up to the truth that his life was in danger. He didn't know how to tell his friends and family, but he was honest with me from the very beginning. There is no reason why he should have told me and not anyone else – save that he knew I could be discreet – but he wanted to tell me, and I listened. To be honest, when he said he wanted to *confide* in me, I just thought he wanted to tell me, privately, how much he had enjoyed working with me. I *never* expected *that* . . .

The next ones to be told exactly what was wrong with Freddie were Joe Fanelli, Jim Beach, Mary Austin and Jim Hutton, who recalled, 'He never liked talking about his illness. From that moment, if anything came on the television to do with AIDS, we would turn over to another channel or switch the set off. It's not that he was unsympathetic towards others with the illness, he simply didn't like being reminded of his fate.' Soon afterwards Freddie would confide in Roger Taylor's girlfriend, Dominique, when she told him that she had breast cancer. For the time being, the other members of Queen were told nothing.

David Wigg had been flown out to Ibiza for Freddie's forty-first birthday bash not in his capacity as a journalist, but as a friend, though he *had* interviewed Freddie and Montserrat about their project. Freddie, however, was unhappy with the finished result of this particular interview, declaring, 'I gave him cream, and all he prints is sour milk.' There was, however, more to it than this, as Wigg explained:

Freddie never knew what a battle I had trying to get the piece in because the editor and deputy editor of the *Express* had got so used to my having access to Freddie that they got a little blasé about his star status. So I asked them for five minutes of their time, and played them the *Barcelona* video. I told them the record would be huge. The deputy editor loved opera – he'd never seen a rock star performing that kind of material before, and that's what made them print the interview. Otherwise they wouldn't have printed anything, and Freddie would have gone mad!'

Aware that time was probably running out, Freddie tried to

ignore his occasional fatigue and set-backs by plunging himself into a number of projects that were not directly connected with his music. The remainder of 1987 was almost exclusively devoted to putting his personal affairs into order, thus ensuring that those friends and lovers, past and present, who were looking after him now would be taken care of after his death. First of all he set about purchasing the Mews, a pair of houses in Logan Mews, the tiny street next to Garden Lodge, which had once been annexed to the house. Converted into a single residence by the Hoare family, the asking price was now a very steep £275,000. Freddie saw the owner just twice: once to clinch the deal and demand immediate vacant possession, and again to hand over the cheque for the full amount with a jocular but firm, 'Here's your money, dear. Now please fuck off!'

Freddie lavished as much attention on his new property as he had on Garden Lodge, spending over £100,000 on renovations and even personally designing a twin-domed conservatory which was to be erected next to it. 'Freddie had many things to achieve before his illness caught up with him,' Jim Hutton said. 'He wanted to leave a little bit of paradise on earth.' Freddie also stocked his pool with around forty half-grown koi carp – £12,000 worth of them – and spent a small fortune having them treated by a specialist later in the year when some of them became ill.

Early in January 1988 Queen entered the Townhouse Studios to begin recording their next album, 'The Miracle'. 'We went into the studio very hungry,' Freddie said afterwards. 'After two years we really wanted to record again.' The inter-group squabbles were still there, too, essential for every album, as Freddie explained, 'You *have* to fight. If it was made *too* easy for me, I would come up with lesser material. *Because* we fight, it makes it much more interesting and you get *la crème de la crème*, the cream of the crop. The fighting for the Queen songs has been one of the worthwhile factors. Some of the ones that were discarded ended up on my solo album. They're good, ha-ha-ha!'

The press, however, were less interested in the album than they were in Queen's personal lives. Only John Deacon escaped the sharp barbs of the tabloids as they served up hefty portions about Freddie's allegedly failing health, Brian May's still persistent denials that he and Anita Dobson were an item, and Roger Taylor's involvement with Debbie Leng, the girl in the highly suggestive Cadbury's Flake television advertisement. The drummer had been going out with the pretty model, sixteen years his junior, for a few months, since she had appeared in one of The Cross's videos. What few were able to comprehend was the somewhat unorthodox manner in which he went about making their relationship more permanent. He married his long-time girlfriend, Dominique Beyrand, on 25 January with Freddie and Mary Austin signing the register as witnesses, then apparently deserted her three weeks later to move into the £700,000 house he had purchased for Debbie Leng and himself.

Initially Taylor told the press that he and Dominique were undergoing a trial separation, and his mother told the *People*, 'The wedding was a love pact because the pair knew their relationship was doomed.' It was, however, Freddie's journalist pal David Wigg who broke the exclusive for the *Daily Express*, drawing the confession, 'I wanted to make a commitment to Dominique and our two children. I wanted to make my children legal and secure. Dominique is a terrific woman. We really are the best of friends.'

The press were also remarkably expedient with their revelations about Leng's past life, claiming that for one so young she had already enjoyed romantic liaisons with five top rock stars, including David Bowie and David Essex, though it was her most recent involvement with the American pop star Simon Climie, of the duo Climie Fisher, which caused her the most hassle a few months later at the Montreux Festival, when Climie and Taylor squared up to one another in the bar of the Hyatt Continental Hotel and almost came to blows. A spokesman for Taylor later attempted to deny that the clash had taken place – unaware that photographs of it had already appeared in the press, along with Climie's complaint about Taylor's 'attitude' and bad language. Freddie found the situation hilarious, and told friends, 'I only wish I could have been there. While they were at it, handbags at thirty paces, I'd have run off with that gorgeous Simon and you wouldn't have seen me for dust!'

On 14 April Freddie appeared alongside Cliff Richard in a special charity performance of *Time* – all the proceeds were donated to the Terrence Higgins Trust, the organization set up in 1982 and named as a tribute to the first known British AIDS victim, to provide information and support for fellow sufferers. Naturally this set the tongues wagging regarding Freddie's own health, particularly when he was observed to have lost a little weight – nothing to do with his condition, as yet, but on account of him recently adopting a stricter diet and cutting down on his intake of vodka.

Freddie's secret almost certainly would have been revealed, however, had it not been for the preventive action taken by one of his friends, a well-known British singer, who spent some time with him before and after the charity performance, and who specifically requested not to be named:

> I was in Freddie's dressing-room. We'd had a few drinks and I was straightening his collar when I noticed a large, dark blotch on one side of his face. He said it was a bruise and that he'd bumped into something at home. I knew otherwise because I'd seen this sort of thing before. Freddie allowed me to cover it with a dab of make-up, then he told me he had AIDS. I was very upset, but he seemed to take it very calmly. He shrugged his shoulders and said, 'It's just one of those things, dear. We've all got to go some time!' Then he swore at me for fussing over him! Two months later when I met him in

Munich, he had more blotches on his arms and neck, and I instinctively knew that this was the beginning of the end.

A few days after the *Time* performance, Freddie flew to Madrid to surprise Montserrat Caballé, who was celebrating twenty-five years in opera with a royal gala at the city's Opera House. As with her recital at Covent Garden, her 'Freddie songs' – by this time an integral act of almost every soirée – were sung at the end of her performance, and it was Freddie who walked on to the stage during her curtain-call to present her with the biggest bouquet she had ever seen in her life.

Montserrat Caballé was not the only *grande dame* in Freddie's professional life at this time. At the beginning of the year he had been approached by Britain's top musical-stage star, Elaine Paige, who was very interested in recording an album of Queen songs. Freddie had known Elaine since 1986 – she had visited Garden Lodge several times and had frequently turned up at his birthday parties with her then partner, Tim Rice. Freddie had loved her definitive portrayal of Eva Perón, and regarded her as 'The English Piaf', which is sad, considering he never lived to see her in the role he said she had been born to play.

Produced by the ubiquitous Mike Moran, who conducted the New Philharmonic Orchestra on six of the ten songs, 'Elaine Paige: The Queen Album' was an innovation, introducing the group's work to a new audience. Freddie would have loved to have sat in on the recording sessions, declaring, 'I like to add my two-penneth, dear!' Moran, however, allowed him access to the studio just once. 'Elaine was putting the vocal on,' he told me, 'and all Freddie did was hold us up for about three hours. So I said, "Well, okay. We've had a nice time, now you'd better piss off and let us get on with some work!"'

The end result of these sessions was breathtaking. Few

serious critics would disagree that when a *chanteuse* of Paige's ability attempts material which they themselves have not created, that material invariably becomes their personal property. Her interpretations of three Queen numbers in particular – *Who Wants To Live Forever?*, *Love Of My Life* and *Is This The World We Created?* – are without any doubt technically superior to Queen's originals, and *Radio Ga-Ga* almost so. One may therefore only lament the fact that there was never a 'Queen Album II'.

On 8 October Freddie and Montserrat Caballé appeared in their most glittering spectacular – again in front of the Spanish royal family – topping the bill at 'La Nit', a huge open-air festival in Barcelona's Montjuich Park. Here, in aid of the International Red Cross, 150,000 fans celebrated the 'Portico', or four-year run-up to the Olympics, which included the ceremonial arrival of the flag from the games' last venue, Seoul. The bill boasted such stalwarts as Dionne Warwick, Earth Wind And Fire, José Carreras, Spandau Ballet, Rudolph Nureyev and Jerry Lee Lewis, and there was an amusing moment when the dreadlocked singer Eddy Grant took to the stage . . . and the royals left their box until he had finished. Freddie and Caballé eclipsed them all, however – even miming – with *Barcelona*, naturally, and two songs from the 'Barcelona' album, due for release two days later: *The Golden Boy* and *How Can I Go On?*, accompanied by Mike Moran, directing the thirty-five musicians flown over from London at Freddie's expense, besides the Barcelona Opera House Orchestra and Choir. To say the evening ended on a majestic note was indeed an understatement.

The reason why the pair mimed to their songs should have been quite obvious to the large contingent of British reporters and was nothing at all to do with a throat infection, as Freddie stated. Most of the audience might even not have known they were miming, had someone had the sense to supply the couple with dummy microphones, and had it not been for the sudden slowing down of the playback tape halfway through the performance. Despite his powerful voice as a rock star, when attempting to sing live with a trained operatic diva – as opposed to having their separately recorded voices doctored by studio technicians – Freddie would have been drowned by both the orchestra and his partner. Also, when the pair were seen in close-up on the television screen, their lip-synchs were nothing short of preposterous – hardly surprising, for Montserrat Caballé had never been expected to mime in her life, and Freddie had only done so under duress for the Montreux Festival and the odd appearance on 'Top of the Pops'.

The press, of course, had a field-day, with Adrian Deevoy of *Q* supplying the most amusingly accurate description of a legend who, in his eyes, had failed to fulfil his duty. Deevoy, who had received a personal backstage pass from Freddie, only to be given short shrift by an armed security guard – the same one who initially refused admittance to Mike Moran, who was Master of Ceremonies! – wrote:

> So what must we do in order to meet Frederick Bulsara, the man for whom the word 'ludicrous' has never been adequate? The unblushing frontperson of Queen who attempted to marry Madame Butterfly to Led Zeppelin while wearing a pink feather boa, having apparently secreted several pounds of root vegetables down his ballet tights. Here he is, the wrist-flicking pianist and melodramatic lyricist whom even Beelzebub couldn't stand the sight of. The macho-moustachioed *bon viveur* who could never decide whether to toss roses to his adoring fans or show them his bottom.

In fact, Deevoy was granted an interview, albeit a brief one, the next day at the Royal Opera House in Covent Garden. The occasion was a lunch-time party to launch the 'Barcelona' album – a brilliant concept which, like the single, the music press hated to a man. 'In those days, the press didn't know what to make of it,' Mike Moran said. 'Later, of course, opera became big time with Pavarotti, the World Cup and the Three Tenors. So suddenly, everybody wants to do a duet with an opera singer. Yet again, Freddie was courageous and before his time.'

Adrian Deevoy's question, as to why Freddie was smoking in view of his alleged throat infection, was met with an archetypically theatrical, 'Oh, do fuck off, dear!' The interview, unfortunately for one usually so adept, was conducted with exactly the same boring questions that the pair had been asked dozens of times already, and attracted the same by now lethargic responses. Once again, Freddie vowed never to speak to the British music press again, and so far as is known, he never did.

9

Love Me Like
There's No Tomorrow

As the new year dawned it was Brian May, not Freddie, whose personal escapades hogged the tabloids, causing him considerable distress, with the sensational news of his split from his wife of thirteen years, Chrissie. '£1m For The Love Of Angie,' yelled the opening blast in the *Sunday Mirror*, voicing the hacks' assumption that the British public knew only the names of the characters in its soap-operas, and not the actors/actresses who played them. From then on, each exclusive divulged how the guitarist had allegedly spent £1 million on a 'farewell' Christmas present (a six-roomed house) for his heartbroken wife, and there was of course the obligatory 'family friend' who occasionally stepped forward to add a juicy titbit and sympathize with May's 'torn feelings'. On the musical side, May suffered further humiliation by not only attending Bad News's dreadful gig at the London Marquee, but by getting on to the stage with fellow guitar legend, Jeff Beck, and jamming with this utter piffle. Earlier, the ensemble had hurled a bucket of water into the audience – to be rewarded by a sudden deluge of pint pots filled with urine. For once, Andrew Smith of *Melody Maker* may have been justified in commenting, 'However hard Bad News might try, they will never be as absurd as the real thing.'

The May–Dobson relationship seemed to have more ups and downs than the proverbial rollercoaster. On the eve of the première of *Budgie*, the press reported that the couple had split because May, unable to cope with not seeing his children on a regular basis, had opted to return to his wife. A few weeks later they were together again at May's Berkshire home, with Dobson lamenting the premature closure of her musical at a loss of over £1 million, and May consoling her with a £42,000 bright-red Mercedes 500 SL convertible. Speaking of the severe depression caused by personal problems, the guitarist opened his heart to Jeff Moses of the American magazine, *RIP*, saying bitterly, 'We've been sheltered. We never had this tabloid thing going on in the past. It's the most awful experience. They just want the dirt. They don't want to know about making music, they want to know if you've been screwing someone else's wife.'

Freddie was ecstatic. For once the press were leaving him alone. Not even when his 'new look' photograph appeared in the *Sunday Times* did the media cotton on to the fact that he had grown his short, stubbly beard to camouflage the lines of illness and the Kaposi's Sarcoma blotches, just beginning to show on his face. 'I just couldn't be bothered to shave any more,' he confessed in the brief editorial. 'It's as boring as slicing bread!'

There was also considerable media interest in Freddie's latest foible – a 144-piece dinner service which had taken ten months to complete, and which set him back a staggering £250,000! Each piece – ranging from the £2,000 each coffee cup to the £5,100 tureen – was hand-painted with miniature copies of Constable masterpieces, edged with gold filigree. One week after purchasing this Freddie and Jim Hutton flew to Geneva, where they spent two days studying the art of porcelain painting with an acclaimed master of the medium, Schira Misrez, before returning to Garden Lodge with four Misrez pieces which had cost £10,000.

What really shocked Freddie's fans, however, was his decision that Queen would not be touring to promote the new album, even though the rest of the group were keen to hit the road again, this time probably visiting China and Russia, but placing particular emphasis on the United States, where they had not had a sizeable hit – single or album – for five years. Two years later, in an interview with the *Daytona Daily News*, Brian May would concede that the Americans could have been put off by the sudden change in Freddie's appearance, adding, 'As soon as he cut his hair, that alienated people. People sometimes don't know where we're coming from.' He was of course making a guarded reference to the country's latent homophobia, and the fact that had it not been for Freddie's arch campness, itself linked to his sexuality, Queen would never have made it anywhere.

Freddie, meanwhile, emphasized in a telephone conversation with Sally Stratton of *Music & Me*, '*I'm* the one who doesn't want to tour, dear. *I* want to change this cycle that we've been going through for so long. If we *do* tour, I want to do it for totally different reasons. I've had enough of these bombastic lights and staging effects. I don't think a forty-two-year-old man should be running around in his leotard any more!' These views would be expressed again on 29 May when, in 'Queen For An Hour', the group's first collective radio interview in almost a decade, they spoke to Mike Reid of Radio One.

Queen's début single from their forthcoming 'The Miracle' album, *I Want It All*, was released on 2 May 1989. It reached Number 3 in the British Charts, and though a relative flop in the United States, it did earn the group the vital air-play which had been lacking in some parts of the country for some time. As another mighty stadium anthem, it was also a big hit across Europe – particularly in Germany, where the video was premièred on a massive screen at half-time during the UEFA Cup Final between Napoli and Stuttgart. With its over-use of huge Xenon Trouper stadium spotlights only highlighting Freddie's bloated appearance, this film was, however, bland by Queen's usual standards. The song itself, otherwise, was a good one and like the others on the album was accredited to all four members of the group – 'So there will be no falling out over who gets the most royalties. Now isn't *that* a good idea!' Freddie told one interviewer – though in certain numbers it is not difficult to ascertain which individual member of the group had influenced them. And not so very long before he had actually commended this individuality, telling a radio interview, 'The trademark of Queen which I like just happens to be a coincidence that there are four writers who write very different material, which gives us maybe a wider span than most other groups.'

Freddie's reluctance to tour was of course linked by the press to his still only alleged physical condition. It was Roger Taylor who was asked the first direct question regarding this – 'Evil voices claim that Freddie has AIDS. Is this true?' – by a German reporter, Götz Kühnmund, while Taylor and May were in Munich promoting the new album. No sensible journalist would have posed so sensitive a question, let alone anticipated an affirmative response, and the drummer was justifiably defensive of his friend, angrily reacting:

What stupidity! Freddie is as healthy as ever and sings better than ever on the new album. We had a party at Brian's a few days ago, and Freddie didn't exactly give the impression he was on his death bed. The reason we're not going to tour is because we can't agree on the whole process. Everything else is just a stupid rumour!

According to Jim Hutton, however, it was at around this time that Freddie told the rest of the group that he was seriously ill, though it is not known if the actual word 'AIDS' came up in the conversation when, in a Montreux restaurant, Freddie 'rolled up his right trouser leg and raised his leg to the table to let the others see the painful, open wound weeping on the side of his calf'. Hutton concluded, 'I think the band had all been well aware that Freddie was seriously ill, and his leg that night was the confirmation they had all been expecting.'

One of Freddie's closest friends, the one who had observed his Kaposi's Sarcoma for the first time, told me that the singer had broken the sad news to the other members of Queen while in Montreux, but dismissed the 'leg-on-table' incident, saying:

> Freddie would never have done anything so crude. It just wasn't his style. And in a restaurant of all places? No, I don't think so! The truth is, he got the band together and said very quietly, 'I suppose you all know what I'm dealing with?' The word AIDS was never used. It wasn't necessary, for their worst fears had already been confirmed by the way he looked, the way he'd been losing weight. Now, of course, they realized that they would eventually lose a very dear friend, and worse still they realized that *their* future was in jeopardy, too. They were terrified of coming to terms with the fact that without Freddie, they would be absolutely nothing, that they would become just another defunct group, which of course has been proved.

'The Miracle', Queen's sixteenth album, was better received than anything the group had done in the last decade, and it was housed in their most appealing cover yet – a computerized four-in-one shot of the group's blended faces, sharing five eyes and an asymmetric haircut. Even the British music press did not disapprove of this chart-topper, though Freddie still burned their reviews the moment he received them. After all the harm and gratuitous insults these people had inflicted in the past, it was too late to redress the balance now.

In America, the album was looked upon as a revelation. 'Mercury has *never* sounded better,' reported *Rolling Stone*, while *Music Express* called it, 'A breathless, frenetic burst of pure energy which takes more twists and turns than a run through the Indy 500'. Brian May had told the magazine, 'I think we'd all die happy if we could just conquer North America again.' The anonymous scribe for *Tracks* wrote, 'Queen are the sort of band who are always there, like buses or the weather. Everyone from American teenagers to German double-glazing salesmen in their forties has either owned a Queen record, seen them play, or behaved foolishly to one of their singles at a disco.'

Maura Sutton, writing for *RAW*, singled out Freddie for particular praise and also hit out at the British music press for its continuous persecution of him: 'Freddie Mercury has always attracted the greatest amount of flak from critics too busy crawling up their own posteriors to recognize the man's tongue-in-cheek self-deprecating witticisms, or to acknowledge the fact that he's one of the greatest rock vocalists *ever*.' The review which excited Freddie the most, however, was the one penned by Chris Welch in *Metal Hammer*, which issued a stern warning to any would-be contenders for the Queen crown:

First there came rock groups. And lo, they were good. And then came Queen, and the world trembled. For Queen are not just a group, they are a way of life, an institution, and they have a place in the national heritage of treasures that means they now transcend all current fashions and styles . . .

Such enthusiasm – and the fact that it was a brilliant album –
enabled 'The Miracle' to reach Number 24 in the American
charts, and again brought up the subject of a possible tour,
which drew the sharp but jocular quip from Roger Taylor,
'The demand for us to tour is getting to be a pain in the ass!'
Brian May was more indignant, however, when speaking to
Chris Welch, this time writing for *Insight*, telling him,
'Freddie just doesn't *want* to tour, so taking the touring side
of things away has really messed up my life – without any
exaggeration. I feel it's taken the whole balance out of my
life.'

In the end Queen's fans had to make do with a video,
albeit an excellent one. *Rare Live – A Concert Through Time
And Space* offered a panorama of the group's on-stage
activities over the last sixteen years, and was principally
aimed at those younger fans who had not been there to
witness their formative years.

Queen's next single, taken from the album and released on
19 June, was *Breakthru*, a fine, bouncy song for which the
group demanded an extra-special video – and a costly one,
for they insisted on the shoot taking place atop a speeding
train. This of course was easier said than done, though the
first stage of the problem was effectively solved by hiring the
privately owned Nene Valley Railway, in Cambridgeshire,
for two days. An old steam train was then 'Queened up' by
having front and side plates fitted and emblazoned with 'The
Miracle Express'. Even the lumps of coal were painted red
and gold!

Initially the railway company refused to allow Queen to be
filmed on top of the train while it was actually moving,
suggesting that the speeding effects be provided by a separate
backdrop, as had happened in some of the old Hollywood
movies. This idea they found boring, so a compromise had to
be reached. The group insured themselves and their
entourage, including Debbie Leng, for £2 million, forking
out a staggering £150,000 for the premium. This, added to

the £200,000 production costs and the £30,000 customizing fee for the train, resulted in *Breakthru* becoming one of the most expensive videos ever made.

The filming took place with 'The Miracle Express' hurtling away at 60 mph on straight stretches of track, putting the fear of God into Freddie who, like everyone else, was only prevented from falling off by a single, rickety-looking iron rail. Afterwards, for the benefit of fans and press photographers who had been tipped off about the secret location by Radio Cambridge, he joked, 'For one moment back there, I thought I'd cashed in my chips!' Asked why he had chosen Debbie Leng, against Roger Taylor's wishes, he replied, 'Because I wanted to make a *sexy* video. And who better to do it than Debbie!'

The single was a bit hit, reaching Number 7 in the charts, and its successor, *The Invisible Man*, peaked at Number 12, though the next two singles – *Scandal* and *The Miracle* itself – did not fare quite so well, just failing to get into the Top Twenty.

Of the videos for these three songs, the one for *The Miracle* was perhaps the most interesting. The group, wishing to appear only at the end of the film, hit on the novelty idea that each of them would be substituted by a junior 'lookalike' wearing identical costume.

At once a series of auditions took place at several London stageschools, and four boys aged between ten and fourteen were chosen from an opening list of 500, a difficult task, for not only were the boys' looks of paramount importance, their miming and impersonation skills had to be spot-on.

'It's Freddie And The Schoolboy Dreamers!' proclaimed one publication, printing photographs of 'John' (James Currie), 'Roger' (Adam Gladdish), 'Brian' (Paul Howard) and 'Freddie' (Ross McCall), posing with the real Queen. Said Freddie of his double, whose previous thespian experience included a spell on the West End stage in *Les Misérables* and the role of the Artful Dodger in a touring production of *Oliver*, 'The resemblance is frightening. Was *I* really *that* good?'

At the beginning of August all the artists involved with 'Live Aid' were asked to pose in Piccadilly's Trocadero for Madame Tussaud's waxworks museum, though as their frontman Freddie was the only member of Queen to be considered. He quite naturally jumped at the idea. Whereas everyone else posed for their models in person, at the last moment, he opted to send a portfolio of photographs because he was worried about anyone getting too close to him in case they began speculating about his appearance. He had started to lose weight, and often felt tired and unwell.

Freddie hit the tabloid headlines again early in November 1989, when the *Sunday Mirror* declared, 'Gay Freddie To Be A "Dad" '. The editorial then went on to explain how Mary Austin was pregnant by an interior designer she refused to name (subsequently revealed to be Piers Cameron), and that Freddie had struck up an amazing love-pact to become a 'father' to the child after telling Mary, 'I love you, but I can't *make* love to you!' Some time before he is alleged to have told a friend, 'A baby? I'd rather have another cat, my dear!' And now, there was another obligatory 'friend' to tell all: 'Mary is fond of the real father but she has no intention of living with him. The main consideration was having a baby. Freddie was always jealous that the rest of the guys in the group had families. He's not at all jealous that Mary went with this other man. They are madly in love, but they are not possessive physically. It was heartbreaking for her when Freddie told her he could not hide his homosexuality any longer, but she has never complained.' The feature, typically, was complemented with a photograph of the couple captioned, 'Gay Godfather – Freddie With Girlfriend Mary'.

That same week Brian May's girlfriend featured in the press – Anita Dobson's most recent project, the television situation comedy 'Split Ends', was about to be axed after just one series. Set in a hairdressing salon, this original, very funny show had contained a contribution from Freddie when, to the tune of *Funiculi-Funicula*, one of the characters had been stopped in his tracks while belting out, 'Whip me, Strip me, Tie me to a tree, Spank me, Wank me, Shoot all over me!'

For Freddie, sadly, there were now far too many days when he was feeling exhausted and ill, and added to his personal distress was the incalculable strain of keeping his tragic secret from the rest of the world. He was regularly visiting his Harley Street specialist, Gordon Atkinson, and when he told Freddie to stop smoking, he did so in a single stroke – quite a feat, for he had been smoking up to forty cigarettes a day since the age of sixteen. The smile, the spirit and the sheer determination of the man, however, showed no signs of fading. He looked positively radiant when he joined the other members of Queen in the television studios as part of Cilla Black's 'Goodbye To The Eighties' – this would be televised on New Year's Eve, when viewers would see the group receiving a *TV Times* award for Best Band of the Eighties. Then, at the end of November, Queen flew to the Mountain Studios in Montreux to begin work on their new album while Freddie still had the strength to sing. It would be their last, and best. As Mary Austin would later explain, 'It was the one thing that gave him much happiness. It made him feel alive inside, through the pain he was experiencing. I think *that* fed the light inside. Each morning there was something else he was working for – it wasn't just taking him to the grave. There was something else he could make happen, and he did.'

On 18 February 1990 Queen were presented with an accolade for Outstanding Contribution to British Music at the British Phonographic Awards. Moreover, while some recipients could not be bothered to collect their awards personally, all four members of the group turned up, looking very smart in their dinner suits. Immediately after the ceremony at the Dominion Theatre, they eschewed the usual celebrity dinner to attend a more important celebration, the twentieth anniversary of Queen – although the current line-up had not been completed until the arrival of John Deacon in 1971, the other three had begun using the name one year earlier.

The group hired Groucho's – a name which appealed to them for obvious reasons – a small club in Soho which they packed with close friends and retainers past and present – just about everyone who had helped, befriended or worked with Queen over the last two decades. The 400 partygoers included Liza Minnelli, Rod Stewart, Michael Winner, Barry Humphries and George Michael. Lata Mangeshkar and Prince Andrew were invited, but could not attend. Each of the guests was greeted by Gina Wildes and Simon Cotton, a Page Three Girl and a Page Seven Hunk from the *Sun*, who added that special 'royal' touch to the occasion by donning guardsmen's uniforms and executing a dapper little drill – before baring their bottoms!

For much of the time, Freddie held court at a table at the back of the club. There was nothing unusual about this, though the press suggested that he was hiding from them, for obvious reasons. Towards the end of the evening a huge cake was wheeled in, decorated with a Monopoly board whose property squares were all Queen hits. The media, however, was only interested in reporting two aspects of the evening: Debbie Leng's £150,000 platinum necklace, given to her by Roger Taylor, and Freddie's appearance. When he was photographed by the *Sun* leaving the club during the early hours of the morning, looking pale and gaunt, and walking rather unsteadily, there was no hiding the fact that here was a very sick man. Even so, he laughed off any suggestion that he was unwell – indeed, what else could he do? – and told one reporter, 'Ill, my dear? I've never felt better!' Later Joe Fanelli rang the newspaper, explaining, 'Freddie isn't poorly. He's lost a little weight, granted, but he needed to because he was getting chubby. He always looks anaemic when he's not wearing his stage make-up. And he *was* a little pissed, like everyone else.' Fanelli's comments were more or less ignored. The press had made up their own minds what to say about Freddie, right or wrong.

A few weeks later, Freddie returned to the Montreux Studios, to resume work on the new album, which was to be called 'Innuendo'. He told Peter Stein of *Top 40*, 'I'm pleased with my vocals on this album. *Innuendo* is a word I often use in Scrabble. For Queen it's a perfect title!' One of the first tracks to be completed was *Delilah*, Freddie's amusing homage to his favourite cat which contained the plum line, 'And then you make me slightly mad when you pee all over my Chippendale Suite.'

This was also a time of soothing, solitary walks along the shore of Lake Geneva, and visits to the quaint little building Freddie had nicknamed 'The Duck House', where he liked to sit in silent contemplation, watching the swans gliding back and forth. Here he wrote a beautiful poem, an ode to the winter he would never see in this his most cherished spot on earth – the only place he could come to to evade the media oppression which was making his life a misery elsewhere. It would take several years, however, for *A Winter's Tale* to emerge – hardly anyone knew it had been written and taped until several years after his death. Listening to it now sends shivers down one's spine.

The 'Innuendo' album, however, was taking longer to complete than anticipated, on account of Freddie's failing health. In June he was fitted with a tiny chest catheter so that his medication could be administered quickly and intravenously – in the studio itself, if necessary – ensuring as little delay as possible.

Such was his strength of will that, while there was breath in his body, he was determined never to give in.

10

Where Is My Star
in Heaven's Bough?

In July 1990, when work of 'Innuendo' transferred to
London's Metropolis Studios, the press became really
troublesome as each morning a near-military-style operation
was mounted to smuggle Freddie out of Garden Lodge
without being seen. Such manoeuvres, naturally, only
attracted more attention, particularly as one or other of his
minders usually yelled some obscenity at the pack of
photographers who tried to rush his limousine.

The ever-faithful Mary Austin later remembered this
harrowing period, saying, 'Freddie was in tremendous pain,
but he forced himself to continue. Working gave him the
courage to face his illness.' The rest of the group and his
entourage closed ranks around him, forming what they
hoped would prove an impenetrable barrier from the press
and scandalmongers. This did not work. During the research

for this book I was told that a journalist thought to be Queen-friendly – being paid by Queen Productions to keep a watchful eye on his colleagues – was actually earning more money by feeding them information. Henceforth, Freddie would scarcely have a waking moment's peace, and a few weeks later the poor man was dealt another terrible blow – one of his most cherished friends, Joe Fanelli, told him that he too was dying of AIDS.

Such was Freddie's concern that his friend should be independent when he was no longer around that, once he had recovered from the shock, he decided to buy Fanelli a place of his own. Very quickly he settled on a small house in Chiswick which was on the market for £160,000, and the estate agent was told to ensure that the owner was not at home when Freddie called to inspect it – though he was recognized by a neighbour. Freddie paid up-front in cash and, as had happened with the Mews, the vendor was told in no uncertain terms to relocate as soon as possible.

Eventually, of course, a photographer, Lee Brooks, of the *Sunday Mirror*, got close enough to Freddie to take a clear picture, and this appeared as an exclusive on 23 September. To be fair, in Brooks's photograph Freddie does not look ill – slimmer, perhaps, but certainly not ill. The giveaway was the way in which he had seemingly shuffled towards his car. There was more consternation, a few weeks later, when he did not turn up at Cliff Richard's fiftieth birthday party, and such was the pressure on Queen by this time that Brian May found himself compelled to inform the press, 'Freddie's okay, but he's been quite rough lately. He definitely hasn't got AIDS, but I think his wild rock'n'roll lifestyle has caught up with him. A lot of the strain has been on him in dealing with the public. I think he just needs a break.'

The crunch came a few days later, when Freddie was snapped with his doctor and friend, Gordon Atkinson, leaving the latter's Harley Street surgery. Wearing a plain grey suit that looked several sizes too big for him, and bent forward, it was clearly an effort for him to cross the street to Atkinson's car. Jim Hutton had bought him a stick, which he had persistently refused to use even about the house, preferring brief work-outs on an exercise cycle. The pair then drove the 150 yards or so to one of Freddie's favourite eateries, Albert Roux's Le Gavroche. And, of course, one hour later the press swooped, though by this time Freddie and Atkinson had left. Interviewed by one journalist, the man who had been sitting at the table next to Freddie remonstrated, 'I never noticed anything. And who *is* this Freddie Mercury, anyhow?' Five minutes and a few hundred pounds later, his story had been amended for the benefit of the tabloids. 'I recognized Freddie at once,' he said. 'He was quite chatty and cheerful, but he looked *awful*.'

The photographer responsible for this and other heartbreaking pictures was twenty-three-year-old Jason Fraser, described by the *News of the World* as 'one of a shadowy group of highly paid, deadly professionals who scour the streets in search of the perfect shots'. For almost a month Fraser had been liaising with contacts, acquiring details of his quarry's every movement outside Garden Lodge – though Freddie was by now a virtual recluse who enjoyed the company of only his closest friends and his beloved cats, emerging every now and then to visit Mary Austin and her son, Richard, who had been born in February. During the afternoon of the shoot Fraser had lain in wait, watching Atkinson's surgery from an upstairs window. He had then trailed Freddie and Atkinson to Le Gavroche taking innumerable pictures with the camera he had concealed under his armpit. Similarly, more candid shots were taken as the pair were leaving.

These photographs had presented Fraser with an unquestionable moral dilemma, and for two whole weeks he had deliberated over what to do with them: destroy them, file them or take the money and expose Freddie's anguish to the whole world. He opted for the latter, earning himself paparazzi notoriety, and many enemies in the Queen camp. Some years later, when it was too late to make amends, Fraser explained that he had only sold the picture – for an alleged five-figure sum – because he hoped that in publishing it he might change the public's perception of AIDS, that as someone famous was dying from the disease – as had happened with Freddie's idol, Rock Hudson – much of the homophobia might stop. He told the *News of the World Magazine* in 1995:

> There was this guy, adored by millions, who had been struck down by a terrible disease that you could get no matter how famous or rich you were. But he was *there*, in the street – *anyone* could have seen him. There's no way I would have broken into a hospital or climbed his garden wall to get my pictures. I saw him, and I admired him. No one, no matter what their sexual preferences might be, deserved what Freddie Mercury got.

To a certain extent, Fraser was right in his opinion. There was considerable sympathy from the general public over Freddie's plight, and that of his fellow sufferers. The attitude of the media, on the other hand, would henceforth become unforgivably ruthless. 'Fraser didn't have any morals at all,' said Jacky Gunn of the Queen Fan Club. 'He was *only* interested in the money. I only hope it did him some good. What he did certainly made Freddie's life a misery.' And Holly Johnson, the Frankie Goes To Hollywood frontman who himself revealed a few years later that he had AIDS, hit out, 'Seeing pictures of Freddie Mercury on the cover of the papers, looking emaciated, that was really *vile*.'

For Queen, meanwhile, it was business as usual. Freddie bravely refused, while he had the strength, to allow his illness to interfere with the group's future plans, even though he might not be there to reap the benefits of what was sown now. Dissatisfied with their American record company,

Capitol, whom they held partly responsible for their slump in popularity in the United States, the group had given Jim Beach instructions to 'sort out a deal' – not an easy task for an act who had not had a major hit in the country for six years. The bargaining factor, however, came when Beach purchased from Capitol the rights to Queen's entire back catalogue. This meant that whoever signed them would be allowed to release their entire output on digitally remastered compact discs for the first time (effectively improving the sound quality of their music, even more so than the British remastering on CD by EMI) and earn everyone involved with Queen a fortune.

In November 1990 a $10 million deal was finalized with Hollywood Records, a fledgeling label started earlier in the year by the multi-million-dollar Walt Disney Corporation. Peter Patermo, the company's president and a huge Queen fan, predicted that their next album would be their biggest ever, and told a press conference, 'Queen are a greatly undervalued asset. It's a great catalogue. I paid a lot of money for it – a Queen's ransom, to be precise – and before too long they're really going to be ruling the charts!'

There was, of course, another sweetener which Hollywood Records could not fail to take into consideration. Freddie Mercury, the soul and essence of Queen, was dying, and everyone knew that most rock legends earned more dead than alive – a sad, but unalterable fact which had been proved far too often.

Amazingly, bearing in mind that most of the tabloids had already drafted Freddie's obituary, it was one of the publications that he despised the most, *Today*, which came up with a suitable defence of the singer on 14 January 1991, the day that the *Innuendo* single was released. The first of a two-part series, 'Freddie Mercury: The Magic and the Mystique', bore the subtitle, 'Crazy Little Thing Called Love Made Me Change My Life', and purported to explain how Freddie had amended his lifestyle since cradling Mary

Austin's son in his arms, on the steps of the church on the day of his christening. Most of the editorial was hogwash, of course – Freddie had never spoken to the newspaper – though the journalist, Richard Middleton, could only be commended for attempting to wean his colleagues away from some of the dreadful stories which had circulated since the publication of the Jason Fraser photograph. According to Middleton, Freddie had given up his daily bottle of vodka, his large intake of rich Indian food, his Rolls Royce and his voracious sexual appetite – all true – and had enrolled with a gym for regular workouts, causing his weight to drop from twelve to nine stone – which was not true at all. Freddie's choice of sexuality – itself entirely normal – was also defended by his friend, Jacky Gunn, who concluded, 'Freddie's a permanent bachelor. He has tried and failed in heterosexual relationships and now realizes that he simply doesn't need to. He jokes that he'd much rather have another cat!'

Few of Freddie's detractors, of course, took the *Today* articles seriously, but it was Paul Prenter, who had neither seen nor spoken to Freddie since being ousted from his circle, who actually shopped him to the press in what may only be described as an act of pure spite. Fearing that there could be reprisals, should he speak again to British reporters, he telephoned the *New York Globe* at the end of January and gave a statement:

> Freddie is just a shadow. His body is frail and stooped and he shuffles along like an old man. He used to be bouncy and vibrant, but now he looks desperately sick. He's lost an alarming amount of weight and his clothes hang on him. No matter what they say officially, he's suffering from something far worse than the flu. I am desperately afraid that it might be AIDS. Freddie has led a very wild life.

Prenter's revelations were printed alongside the Jason Fraser photograph, and headed, 'AIDS Ravages Rocker Queen'. It was ironic that, within a few months, Prenter too would succumb to the disease.

To a certain extent Freddie took much of his frustration out on some of his friends. Peter Straker and Barbara Valentin were among the first to fall by the wayside, as David Evans pointed out to me:

> There's a condition called AIDS-anger, where those who are terminally ill get terribly angry for no reason. It's an anger which goes with the fact that these people are alive, and you're going to die. Barbara and Straker fell under that particular shadow because they were unable to handle his anger. Freddie cut out a lot of people at the end of his life, especially the ones who had lived with him through his hectic, wild years. He couldn't cope with the people who only adored him as that boisterous, partying, devil-may-care person. He was in incredible pain for the final twelve months of his life, yet he still had to try and keep going. So, he gathered about him only the people he knew would sustain his soul, the ones he could keep up with in terms of the old days.

Innuendo, the single, entered the British charts at Number 1 – the first time Queen had occupied the top slot since 1981, when they had done so with *Under Pressure*. In America, however, fickle radio stations dictated that it would not be prudent to release a song of over six minutes' duration, so Hollywood Records plumped for *Headlong* – a wise choice, for it peaked at Number 3. The 'Innuendo' album itself came out three weeks later – again, it went straight to Number 1, selling 250,000 copies in its first week alone, annoying the British music press, who had unanimously reviled it.

In the United States, the album was released on 5 February in a fanfare of typically Hollywoodian publicity. The

$400,000 launch took place aboard the *Queen Mary*, the 81,000-ton Cunard–White Star liner which had recently been purchased by the Walt Disney Corporation and turned into a hotel. Permanently moored in concrete, it stood next to Howard Hughes's famous plane, *Spruce Goose*, in Long Beach, California. The 1700 guests marvelled at the Queen performance staged by illuminated robots, which proved so popular that it had to be repeated, and the evening was rounded off with one of the most impressive firework displays California had ever seen when $100,000 worth of them were let off to the strains of *Bohemian Rhapsody*. But whereas Brian May and Roger Taylor turned up for the party, John Deacon and Freddie did not – one citing 'family reasons', the other saying parties were no longer his scene. This infuriated the executives of Hollywood Records, one of whom hit out, 'This company has invested $10 million in those four – they should *all* be here, family or no family.' And when asked for his opinion, Michael D Eisner, the Walt Disney chairman, shrugged his shoulders and added, 'This wasn't just a party for *Queen*. It was a coming out party for the label.'

Although 'Innuendo' only reached Number 30 on the *Billboard* album chart, Hollywood Records were far from disappointed. After six years in a virtual rock wilderness, Queen were back.

The covers for the album and the four singles extracted from it contained a series of pencil drawings by the early nineteenth-century illustrator, Grandville, hand-coloured and only slightly amended by Richard Gray. The one used for the album was entitled 'A Juggler Of Universes', and depicted a shock-haired clown doing just that, though the addition of a banana was Freddie's idea.

The well-known rock photographer, Simon Fowler, was commissioned to take the group's publicity shots, though of the hundred or so, only three were seen by fans because the others were deemed 'unsuitable' by Queen Productions. One of them looking somewhat elongated, and another of them lying horizontally on individual shelves is thought to have been thus arranged so that Freddie's quite drastic weight loss might not be so readily discernible. The third shot depicted him sitting unusually apart from the other three. The media speculation that he had been touched up to make him appear healthier, however, was hotly refuted by Queen's publicist and agent, Roxy Meade, who only added to the confusion and intrigue by saying of the photographs, 'The problem is the technique used, where only half of them are in focus at any one time,' and of the group's immediate plans, 'There's no chance of them doing interviews or going on TV. I'm waiting for the video to be finished.'

Grandville's drawings also formed the basis for the £120,000 *Innuendo* video, brought to life on the screen by the animator Jerry Hibbert, winning him an American 'Gold Camera' award. A six-and-a-half-minute Grand Guignol masque, it also featured a fandango with plasticine figures, animated sketches of the group, and film clips of the Nuremberg Rally, the funeral of Freddie's former singing idol Oum Kalthoum, and battle footage from the Second World War – the latter replaced at the last moment by fragments of Hungarian folk-dancing when, unexpectedly, war broke out in the Gulf.

In the United States Hollywood Records capitalized on the Gulf War by issuing a limited edition CD to the troops – President Bush's victory speech, superimposed over Queen's *We Are The Champions*. This was allegedly to compensate for the BBC's so-called 'War And Peace' list which recommended that songs such as *Another One Bites The Dust* – for obvious reasons extremely popular in the Gulf – Billy Joel's *We Didn't Start The Fire*, and even John Lennon's *Give Peace A Chance* should not be played for the duration of the conflict.

The fact that the *Innuendo* video did not contain footage of Queen themselves, of course, only supplemented the rumours that Freddie really was too ill to be seen by his fans. For this reason he insisted on making a personal appearance in the video for the next single, *I'm Going Slightly Mad*, which was filmed by the Torpedo Twins at London's Limehouse Studios in the middle of February. The media, of course, awaited the outcome of this with bated breath.

This song was rich with Freddie's camp, puckish humour, a colonial trait described by Roger Taylor as 'Noël Coward meets Oscar Wilde meets Led Zeppelin', and the amusing, largely monochrome video suited this to a T. The entire £200,000 escapade was engineered by Freddie himself. Stopping every few minutes to issue instructions to his team and to rest, he wore a £900 shaggy wig and lots of pancake make-up to impersonate Lord Byron, pronounced classic lines such as 'I think I'm a banana tree!', and cavorted with live penguins and a man in a gorilla suit – while John Deacon gurned in a joker's hat and played with a yo-yo, Roger Taylor wore a steaming kettle on his head and rode a tricycle, and Brian May dressed as a penguin with a large yellow beak and silver fingernails. Freddie then traded his poet's garb for a stunning blue and yellow swansdown and ostrich-feather redingote. A masterpiece!

The video shoot was not without drama when, at a crucial moment one of the penguins – Cleo, who Freddie took to and fussed over like a baby, mindless of his agony – urinated on the sumptuous leather sofa, missing him by inches. 'The Day A P-P-P-Penguin Decided To Go For A P-P-P-Pee,' ran the headline in the *People*, harking back to the famous television commercials for the chocolate bar of the same name. Freddie told Kate Molloy, 'I wanted to make this video as memorable as possible. I've always wanted to co-star in a video with a gorilla and a group of penguins. A little bit of Queen madness is wanted right now, so don't bother to question our sanity!'

The press, however, were unconvinced that Freddie was not ill. At the end of April he was reported to be receiving round-the-clock medical attention, virtually bedridden, and slowly losing his sight. Even so, such was this man's unique strength of will that by early May he and the rest of Queen were beavering away in the Mountain Studios on their next album. It would be here, towards the end of August, that Freddie would record his final song, *Mother Love*, a truly beautiful pastiche which contained one line which we now know had become his credo:

I long for peace before I die . . .

But had the troubled, persecuted young man found such a thing in this once-unloved haven, far from the prying eyes of an increasingly menacing media? Brian May happened to think so, as he told a radio interviewer shortly afterwards, 'He tried for the high notes, paused, downed a couple of vodkas, and got it right. He could hardly stand on account of his pain, yet I never once saw him put his head in his hands and say he'd had enough.' And Roger Taylor said in the same interview, 'The last thing he wanted was to draw attention to any kind of weakness or frailty. He didn't want any kind of pity.'

Freddie had recently purchased a three-bedroomed penthouse in Montreux, with extensive views of the lake and city, and he had hired some of the best – and costliest – interior designers in Switzerland to make the place 'homely', tragically for no other reason than spending for spending's sake, for he had already decided that he had had enough. Wishing to end the struggle – according to Jim Hutton, who now broke the news that he too was HIV positive – Freddie had decided to stop taking his medication.

Yet in England Brian May's secretary was following instructions and telling the press, 'Freddie is absolutely fine. He has been going to auctions every day for the last week.'

Just ten weeks after *I'm Going Slightly Mad*, Queen released another single, *Headlong*, which many fans found considerably less appealing than the B-side of the CD single, *Mad The Swine*. Freddie had written this song some twenty years previously for one of Queen's albums; it had been recorded in 1972, but never used until now.

On 30 May Freddie, Roger Taylor and John Deacon spent most of the day in the studio with Rudi Dolezal, filming the video for their next American single, *These Are The Days Of Our Lives*. Brian May was still promoting 'Innuendo' in the United States and would film his contribution a little later. The video was to complement a television documentary, 'Days Of Our Lives', charting the Queen story for their new generation of fans. Freddie was distressed, however, to learn that its narrator was Axl Rose, of the heavy rock group, Guns 'N' Roses. Over the past few years he had issued a number of extremely unpleasant anti-gay, racist statements to the media, and one of Freddie's long-standing ambitions had been to meet him, and spit in his eye.

The *These Are The Days Of Our Lives* video, sadly, was also Freddie's way of saying goodbye to his fans, his very last piece of film, which ends with the half-whispered, heartfelt words, 'I still love you!'

In Britain Queen's next single was *The Show Must Go On*, without any doubt the most moving, portentous song Freddie ever performed. *Everything* about it pointed towards that final, now unstoppable curtain. 'My make-up may be flaking, but my smile stays on,' he defiantly opines, before committing himself to the inevitable. 'I'll face it with a grin, I'm never giving in!' Few men could have faced up to their fate with such blatant, almost self-parodying courage. This is what made Freddie Mercury so very special to so many people, and this is why this particular *chanson réaliste* will always remain my favourite.

The single, released on 14 October, would be Queen's last to be issued in Freddie's lifetime. It was followed, two weeks later, by Queen's second compilation album, 'Greatest Hits II', which gave them their eighth Number One and which was complemented by a *Greatest Flix II* video.

When Freddie returned to Garden Lodge early in September 1991 after visiting his Swiss flat, he had to be secreted into the grounds via the entrance to the Mews, in the back of a friend's car. That same day he was seen at home by Dr Brian Gizzard, the head of the AIDS unit of London's Westminster Hospital. The press, having been tipped off that it was only a matter of time, refused to let him be. Sometimes there would be as many as seventy reporters and photographers hanging around the perimeter of the building, like vultures. Some climbed the walls or perched their tripods on ladders, training their lenses on the upstairs windows for the slightest movement.

Towards the end of the month, Montserrat Caballé, who since Freddie had told her of his illness had called him at least once every week, now rang to say that she was coming to London for a recording session. Freddie begged her not to put herself through the ordeal of going to the house. She told me:

> I was in London to record the aria 'Christine' from *Phantom of the Opera* – I was doing it for him because he loved it, so I rang him from the studio and played it down the phone. He was both happy and sad. Happy that I had done this just for him, sad that we would never see each other again, and as I put the phone down, I said to myself, 'What a brave, wonderful man this is.'

Friends and loved ones who did visit Garden Lodge were jostled and interrogated, particularly Mary Austin and Dave Clark who with Jim Hutton, Joe Fanelli and Peter Freestone took it in turns to sit at Freddie's bedside. On one occasion Hutton threatened to thump an aggressive reporter; on another Roger Taylor was blinded by the popping flashbulbs and drove his car into the back of one of the ever-present police cars. The tension also deepened the rift which had apparently been developing for some time between Mary Austin and Jim Hutton – particularly when, according to Hutton, Mary had suggested that Freddie should remove his wedding ring because she felt it might cause him discomfort if his fingers suddenly began swelling, as he approached the end.

For Hutton, who spent more time with Freddie than anyone during these final days, this was a trip to Calvary, as he recalled, 'I often used to cry on my own, but I made sure Freddie never saw me upset. Throughout the day, for him I'd be strong, but his dying face haunted my nights, and I'd always end up crying myself to sleep . . .'

At midnight, on 23 November, it was Freddie himself who ended all the speculation by issuing a statement which stunned not just his millions of fans, but his friends also:

Following the enormous conjecture in the press over the last two weeks, I wish to confirm that I have tested HIV positive and have AIDS. I felt it correct to keep this information private in order to protect the privacy of those around me. However, the time has come for my friends and fans around the world to know the truth, and I hope that everyone will join with me in the fight against this terrible disease.

The sad news made the front pages of just about every newspaper in the world – even in Russia and China, where Queen had never played. Yet even as Freddie's fans were choking back their tears and trying to take this in, newsflashes were pronouncing even grimmer tidings. At 7.01 p.m. on Sunday 24 November 1991, the greatest rock star and showman of his generation had passed away.

Freddie was only forty-five years old and just weeks before, in his last known interview, he had told the *Daily Express*, 'I don't really think about when I'm dead, or how they are going to remember me. I don't really think about it. It's up to them. When I'm dead, who cares? I don't!'

11

Till the End of Time . . .

It is not the purpose of this book to enlarge on Freddie's final, agonizing hours. These were recorded three years after his death by Jim Hutton in clinical, distressing – and some of the singer's close friends have alleged – greatly exaggerated detail. One of these, who cannot be named for legal reasons, particularly demanded that the record be set straight:

> That part of the story, where he was with Freddie, is very inaccurate. Jimmy wasn't even in the room, and all that about Freddie's leg breaking is nonsense. Peter Freestone *was* in the house, but he wasn't in the room either. The *only* person with Freddie when he died was Dave Clark, and he phoned me as soon as it happened. All the other stories are lies.

Although Freddie had been critically ill, the end did come sooner than anyone had anticipated. Dave Clark was the first

180

to submit to a press interview. Fighting back the tears, he said, 'For me he was a rare gem, a rare painting. He was a rare person, but he suffered and when he slipped away, I knew he was going to a better place.' Mary Austin, who had spent the day at Garden Lodge – only to leave ten minutes before Freddie died, promising that she would be back the next morning – had the harrowing task of informing the Bulsaras. She said, 'He faced his illness with incredible bravery, but he did suffer, mentally and emotionally, as well as physically. His mother saw him eight days before he died, but he became very ill very quickly, and he really didn't want them [his parents] to see him.'

Queen's publicist, Roxy Meade, issued a brief statement to the effect that Freddie had died as the result of bronchial pneumonia, brought on by AIDS. Brian May, speaking on breakfast television, also praised his friend's courage, and defended Freddie's decision to tell the world the truth concerning his illness. 'It would have been very easy to put on his death certificate just "pneumonia", and it could have side-stepped everything,' the guitarist declared. 'But he said, "I have got this and there is no shame, no stigma." '

Later in the day the remaining members of Queen issued their own statement, part of which read, 'We feel over-whelming grief that he has gone, sadness that he should be cut down at the height of his creativity, but above all great pride in the courageous way that he lived and died. It has been a privilege for us to have shared such magical times.' May also composed a moving letter, which he published in the fan club's Christmas magazine, thanking Freddie's admirers for their love and support – an affection which would not simply flourish, but escalate. (Two years later Mary Austin would convey a message to the fans in the same magazine: 'With the terrible stigma associated with AIDS, you [the fans] have shone through. You didn't turn away, you saw the man beyond the disease, loved him through it, despite it and beyond it . . . By your continued loyalty to Freddie you help lift the spirits of others, also affected.')

Montserrat Caballé, absolutely heartbroken, sobbed, 'I'm beside myself with grief. I loved Freddie as a friend and I respected him as a musician and composer. I knew he was dying, and I bitterly hoped he would be cured. Freddie was a very tough person. He always used to tell me that he had to make his own way in life, carrying his own luggage.' Then, referring to the aria from *Phantom of the Opera*, which she had dedicated to him, she added, 'There is one line in that song – "I hope you are here in some way another time" – which will always remind me of my lovely Freddie.'

Kenny Everett, who himself succumbed to AIDS a few years after Freddie, offered a typically zany tribute, but heartfelt all the same: 'He was a genius. But I won't be going to his funeral. After all, Freddie won't be there!' There was another back-handed compliment from James 'Trip' Khalaf, the soundman on Queen's tours between 1976 and 1986, who said, 'Freddie had no marketable skills, so what else could he have been but a huge, bombastic rock star? And the son-of-a-bitch did a great job!'

The backlash, of course, began at once, as hundreds of fans queued up outside Garden Lodge to pay their last respects – not in the conventional sense as with other legends, being allowed into the domicile and filing past the catafalque, but simply by being there, while radio stations across the globe were playing Freddie's records virtually non-stop. The broadsheets proffered respectable eulogies, though the tabloids would only give Freddie's musical skills second place after his sexual exploits in what must certainly be some of the most poisonous pieces of journalism since the death of Rudolph Valentino back in 1926. A typical article would begin, 'This is not a moral judgement...' before launching into a tirade of insults which in most cases was totally unnecessary and often hypocritical. None is worth repeating in this book.

Initially Freddie was championed by Virginia Bottomley,

the Minister of Health, who applauded him for the bravery of his announcement, adding that this would now 'encourage others to recognize the dangers of the disease and practise prevention'. Dr Patrick Dixon, the founder of the charity AIDS Care Education and Training, spoke out in his defence, saying, 'His behaviour *did* change, but not in time to prevent his own death. The media should now concentrate on helping to prevent *more* HIV infection, not on harassing people who are vulnerable.'

By far his staunchest defence, however, came from Terry Sanderson in his powerful 'Mediawatch' pages in *Gay Times*, whose blistering condemnation of the tabloids began with a borrowed phrase from the veteran journalist Woodrow Wyatt: 'We're badly served by our broadcasting and press commentators. Most are too stupid or too lazy to examine the facts behind the issues.' Admitting to me how Freddie had probably caused problems for himself by not issuing his statement until it was almost too late, Terry explained why some sections of the press had singled out Freddie in particular for their hate campaign:

AIDS hysteria was past its peak, but it was still powerful enough for the press to need a focus, and Freddie provided it. From the tabloids' point of view, he died just at the right moment. He was perceived by them as a standard homosexual – promiscuous and uncaring about health and safety. That's how uneducated many of them were and still are.

Jim Hutton always maintained that Freddie had never wanted to make a statement, that he had only allowed Jim Beach to persuade him to release it so as to prevent the tabloids from acquiring another scoop. He wrote in his book, 'It was Freddie's way of saying to those so eagerly awaiting his death, "Fuck you!"' Others have said that he was too ill to be aware of his surroundings, let alone

sufficiently coherent to dictate any statement; that, had he
wanted the world to know the precise details of his illness, he
would have spoken out some time before – as Rock Hudson
had done – and attracted considerably more media
sympathy.

David Evans, on the other hand, shared the same theory as
many of Freddie's friends: 'Freddie couldn't *afford* to make
anything public, not for selfish reasons but for Queen's sake
and for the sake of their wives, children and employees. He
was terrified of what the public's reaction would have been
towards *them*.' And Mary Austin added, defensively, 'It took
him a long, long time to accept for himself that he had AIDS,
so how could he tell the world when he couldn't accept it
himself?'

Alas, the truth may now never be known.

Freddie's funeral, during the afternoon of 27 November at
West London's Kensal Green Crematorium, was a subdued,
dignified and essentially private affair, attended by thirty or
so close friends and fourteen members of his family – most of
whom had not seen him for years. The funeral and the
family-only ceremony which had preceded it earlier in the
day were conducted entirely in the Zoroastrian faith.
Freddie's parents, among the handful of mourners there not
wearing black, had insisted on this. The chanting by two
white-robed priests, calling for the soul of the departed to be
transported to *qaroghman bahest*, or eternal heaven, was
almost entirely in Avasta, an ancient language of the Parsees.
Only the words, 'sit' and 'stand' were pronounced in English.

Mary Austin was escorted into the chapel by Dave Clark,
who had travelled with her in the first car, replacing Jim
Hutton at the last moment. Hutton, Peter Freestone and Joe
Fanelli were relegated to the third car, behind Jim Beach.
'The three of us felt let down,' Hutton later said, claiming
that Mary had deliberately snubbed him by failing to
recognize his next-of-kin status. 'We'd been the ones with

Freddie through thick and thin during his illness. It seemed that no sooner was he dead than we were being pushed aside.' Within the chapel, however, Clark moved to another pew so that these three could sit with Mary at the front.

Mary's wreath was inscribed, 'For my dearest with my deepest love, from your old faithful.' Brian May's and Anita Dobson's read, 'Dear Freddie, we will love you forever,' while Roger Taylor's bore a simple, 'Goodbye old friend, peace at last.' Jim Hutton sent a swan made of white flowers, with a lengthy poetic message which concluded, 'You died as you lived – everyone's friend.' Elton John, who wept unconsolably throughout the twenty-minute service, sent a heart of one hundred salmon roses which he had inscribed, 'Thank you for being my friend.' In all there were more than 400 floral tributes from around the world, conveyed to Kensal Green by five Daimlers. They were subsequently donated to several local AIDS hospices.

Freddie's oak coffin, adorned with a single red rose, was transported from the Rolls Royce hearse into the chapel to the strains of Aretha Franklin's *Precious Lord Take My Hand*. A little later Montserrat Caballé's recording of Verdi's *D'amor sull'ali rosee*, from *Il Trovatore*, was relayed through loudspeakers. These were arguably the only sections of the ceremony Freddie would have approved of, for he had rejected his faith long ago.

There was also a moment which would have amused him, as a cat lover, when a large black tom unceremoniously nudged its way through the cortège.

It was over.

Epilogue

Mona Lisa Just Keeps on Smiling

With 'Greatest Hits II' still clinging to the top of the album charts, *Bohemian Rhapsody* was re-released as a double A-side with *These Are The Days Of Our Lives* on 9 December. Precisely fifteen years after it had first topped the charts, it did so once more, remaining at the top for five weeks. Most importantly, it earned over £1 million in royalties, money which was donated to the Terrence Higgins Trust. Brian May and Roger Taylor presented the cheque to the organization in April 1992, at the Ivor Novello Awards. Freddie had won a posthumous award for the best-selling A-side of 1991, and May an award for best television commercial theme for 'Driven By You', written for Ford Cars. The first single from his début album, 'Back To The Light', had ironically been released the day after Freddie's death. The most successful solo project thus far in May's

186

career, the single reached Number 6 in the charts. Roger Taylor told the audience at the ceremony, 'The best way to fight this appalling illness is to make sure everybody knows about AIDS and *how* it can be fought. Freddie's best-known song has helped do that.'

In the United States the re-released *Bohemian Rhapsody* got to Number 2 in the charts, with all the proceeds going to the Magic Johnson AIDS Foundation. This was something Freddie may not have approved of, according to the 'out' tennis player Martina Navratilova, who launched a vicious attack on the famous baseball star who had recently declared himself HIV positive, attracting a huge amount of the public sympathy which had been denied Freddie – simply because Johnson had admitted that he had caught the virus after sleeping with hundreds of women.

What promised to be the ultimate tribute to Freddie, 'A Concert For Life: The Freddie Mercury Concert For AIDS Awareness', took place at Wembley Stadium on Easter Monday, 20 April 1992, with the surviving members of Queen joining what the promoters vowed would be 'a host of stars' on the hugest stage the venue had seen since Queen's last concerts in the summer of 1986.

The tabloids, of course, questioned the theme of the proposed show. 'AIDS *awareness*' posed the *Daily Mail*'s Toby Young. 'That was a little odd considering Freddie Mercury didn't make the world aware that he was suffering from AIDS until twelve hours before he died of it.' Even so, all 72,000 tickets for the event sold out in just four hours, before the final guest-list was announced, and such was the hype that many forecast another 'Live Aid'.

Unfortunately, much of the concert comprised barely second-rate entertainment hardly worthy of an artist of Freddie's calibre. Elaine Paige had not been invited to give the concert a touch of class, nor had representatives from pop's camp element much loved by Freddie, such as Boy George, or Erasure, to make it sparkle, Montserrat Caballé *had* been asked to appear, but her punishing schedule would not accommodate an extra engagement. 'I was in Seville for Expo '92,' she told me, 'And I asked if I could take part via satellite. Unfortunately, they couldn't make the connection. I was very upset because I was singing in *La Galliarda*, an opera which Freddie had loved. Still, I *was* with him in spirit.'

The comparative amateurism of the concert was inadvertently highlighted by the producers of the live televised event when they played video and film clips of the real thing between acts: Freddie Mercury, proving ultimately that he had possessed qualities they had only dreamed of, namely showmanship and charisma. Neither did the concert raise any inordinate amount of money for its intended charity, certainly not in relation to its size. Of the £2 million grossed in ticket sales, 1¼ million was deducted for 'production costs' alone.

The Boston-based ensemble, Extreme, excelled with their Queen rock-medley, but their tuneless rendition of *Love of My Life*, the song Freddie had once dubbed his 'Hymn à l'Amour', left a great deal to be desired. Def Leppard, Guns 'N' Roses, Metallica, Paul Young and Roger Daltrey succeeded only in making a lot of noise and completely failed to resurrect any of the magic associated with Freddie. Toby Young, again writing for the *Daily Mail*, denounced Annie Lennox's spot as 'a masterpiece of stupidity', and her duet of *Under Pressure* with David Bowie as 'tawdry'. Bowie himself was criticized for his somewhat boastful comment, referring to his hedonistic days on the same tour-circuit as Queen, 'We all used to play the same dance-halls and theatres . . . we slept with a lot of the same people, too.' Bowie was also criticized by A N Wilson of the *Daily Telegraph* for sinking to his knees and reciting an unconvincing if not ludicrous Lord's Prayer.

The shock item on the bill had to be Guns N' Roses, a group which Freddie had positively loathed. In 1988 one of their songs had contained the unpleasant line, 'Immigrants and faggots spread disease' – a line which Freddie believed had been directed at him personally – since which time their concerts had constantly been heckled by gay rights activists. Their frontman Axl Rose received so many threats before the Wembley show that it was widely rumoured that he would pull out of the proceedings, particularly when he failed to turn up for rehearsals. Now, as he took to the stage, he received the vitriol he deserved from Freddie's many gay fans, and Richard Smith of *Gay Times*, curiously writing in the present tense, observed:

> When they play, a threatened protest is inaudible above the deafening cheers. Elton John puts his arm around Axl Rose, a gesture caused perhaps less by an uncontrollable groundswell of affection than that this is what one does at such events. Whatever, Axl looks extremely uncomfortable. It's unlikely that he's the only person in that vast stadium who loved Freddie but hated faggots.

Lisa Stansfield and George Michael on the other hand were sheer perfection – she 'vacuuming' the stage with *I Want to Break Free*, he with *Somebody to Love*, and together with an absolutely sublime *These Are the Days of Our Lives*.

George Michael was so good, in fact, that rumours soon began circulating that he would become Queen's new frontman, a role which he would never have dreamed of accepting, for it would not have been tolerated by Freddie's admirers. 'That concert was the proudest moment of my career,' he later reflected, sporting the silver and red rhinestones AIDS symbol brooch presented to him by Elizabeth Taylor. 'I was living out a childhood fantasy.' Elton John too offered a powerhouse performance – one Freddie would have been proud of – with *The Show Must Go On*. Liza Minelli, on the other hand, merely struggled with the band and a full cast through a penultimate *We Are The Champions*, before Freddie himself rounded off the event on the big screen, in all his regal, ceremonial glory, while the entire stadium erupted into an exuberant *God Save The Queen*.

The heroes of the evening, however, had to be the trio of May, Deacon and Taylor, and Elizabeth Taylor. 'Freddie was denied the privilege of growing old,' Brian May said. 'But in forty-five years he packed in enough living for a dozen lifetimes.' Accompanying himself on the piano he then sang a tremulous *Too Much Love Will Kill You* with such intense emotion that one can only wonder at how much sorrow one man can shoulder without breaking down. There were absolutely no exceptions – he completely overshadowed everyone.

Elizabeth Taylor, despite being heckled by a group of Guns 'N' Roses fans – 'I'll *get off* in a minute. I have something to say!' – was also clearly on the verge of tears. The undisputed champion of the gay man, gay rights and AIDS awareness for nearly half a century she had offered solace to the troubled psyches of Montgomery Clift, James Dean, Michael Jackson and Rock Hudson to name but a few – in the latter's case when he had been dying from AIDS. She had also raised over $10 million for AIDS charities in one month alone.

In a lengthy unscripted speech, Elizabeth Taylor now urged the world to practise safe sex and syringe-sensibility. She concluded:

We are here to celebrate the life of Freddie Mercury, an extraordinary rock star who rushed across our cultural landscape like a comet shooting across the sky. We are also here to tell the whole world that he, like others we have lost to AIDS, died before his time. The bright light of his talent still exhilarates us, even now that his life has been so cruelly extinguished. It needn't have happened –

it shouldn't have happened. Please, let's not let it happen again.

The opera world paid its own, perhaps more stylish, tribute to Freddie on 28 June, in a gala at the Banqueting House in London's Whitehall. It was organized and stage-managed by Peter Freestone, the man who had taught Freddie more or less all he knew about the medium, and it comprised a performance of his favourite opera, *Il Trovatore*. Montserrat Caballé, the patron of the English Chamber Opera Touring Company which performed it, announced to the press, 'This gala is a fitting tribute by the opera community to a great composer and performer who is an immense loss to all spheres of music. I miss him very much.'

The proceeds from this concert were donated to the Mercury Phoenix Trust, the organization founded in Freddie's honour with the profits from the Wembley tribute – not just from ticket sales but from broadcasting, record and video rights. The trustees were Brian May, Roger Taylor, Mary Austin and Jim Beach. John Deacon refused his trusteeship. Indeed, he had taken a lot of persuading to appear in the Wembley show, and has since played a minor role in other homages to Freddie because, it is alleged, he does not approve of the hype involved and prefers to remember his friend in his own way.

Up to and including the fifth anniversary of Freddie's death, the Mercury Phoenix Trust has raised a colossal £5 million for AIDS projects based in Britain, Holland, Mexico, India, Thailand and Uganda. The Freddie Mercury Hospice, widely reported in the press during the summer of 1992, is still waiting to be built.

Freddie did not leave as much money as most people expected. In his last will, sealed just seven days before his death, and with Jim Beach and John Libson (his accountant) as executors, he left gross assets amounting to just over £8½ million. A huge portion of his wealth had been spent on medical care, largely at the Westminster Hospital, during the last years of his life. He had also bought Jim Hutton a house in Ireland, and anonymously donated £500,000 to AIDS research.

The main beneficiary, not surprisingly, was the loyal Mary Austin, who received half of his estate, plus whatever share of Queen's publishing and recording royalties would have gone to Freddie over the next fifty years, plus Garden Lodge and the Mews which alone were valued at £4 million. A further 25 per cent went to Freddie's sister, Kashmira Cooke, and the remaining 25 per cent was bequeathed to his parents, something of a surprise, for they had always rejected Freddie's generosity, and in an earlier will had been left not one penny. Jim Hutton, Joe Fanelli and Peter Freestone each received £500,000, and £100,000 went to Freddie's chauffeur, Terry Giddings. There were, surprisingly again, no other legatees, and nothing was left to charity. In his lifetime Freddie had given millions to needy causes, but in death he was concerned only in providing for his loved ones.

It had been Freddie's wish that the trio of Hutton, Freestone and Fanelli remain at Garden Lodge for as long as they desired. One was dying, another soon would be. Unfortunately, this particular instruction had not been set down in writing, and just one week after Freddie's funeral, Mary Austin gave them twelve weeks' notice to leave her property. Not only that, but while finding alternative accommodation, all three were compelled to move into the Mews while the Garden Lodge security system was reviewed and guards posted on duty, twenty-four hours a day.

Mary told David Wigg at the time of the men's eviction:

It was always going to be awkward, and it would have been impossible for Jimmy to stay. Jimmy's relationship with Freddie was not one I could totally appreciate, so it left me at an advantage. He was let down a lot by boyfriends. He'd become a star and people went for the trappings rather than looking at the heart. And Freddie had an enormous heart.

Jim Hutton lodged with friends until the end of May, when he received his inheritance and was able to purchase a small house in Stamford Brook. He now spends much of his time in Ireland. Joe Fanelli returned to America, where he died the following year.

Mary Austin still lives at Garden Lodge, which has been described as a cross between an impenetrable fortress and a mausoleum by the few outsiders who have had the privilege of entering its portals. One told me, 'Freddie's bedroom is exactly the same now as it was the day he died. Not one item has been moved, and everything is covered in dust. It's sad to think of how he loved all the things in that room, of what he would think if he went back there now.' Mary lives with her two children – James, her second son, was born early in 1992. Her relationship with Piers Cameron did not survive her turbulent, well-trained-for transition from personal assistant and girlfriend to *châtelaine*.

On the eve of the Wembley tribute, Mary had given her only in-depth interview, to David Wigg of the *Daily Express*. Admitting that five months after losing Freddie she was still unable to cry, she had confessed publicly exactly what those closest to him had known for years:

> Even in death I care about him and hope he's okay. I felt married to Freddie. It was for better or for worse. We had nothing when we met, so it was for richer and for poorer. And we stayed together when he was sick, so it was in sickness and in health and until death us do part.

Soon after reading this moving testimony, Jim Hutton decided to 'put the record straight', and with the help of a journalist named Tim Wapshott began compiling *Mercury And Me*, an account of his several years as Freddie's 'husband', which was also his way of asserting his claims as the singer's 'widow'. John Dugdale of the *Sunday Times* labelled him 'the Sally Burton to Austin's Elizabeth Taylor'.

The result was a highly readable book with a pleasing mixture of pathos and camp, though cynics, susceptible third parties and, most importantly, several of Freddie's friends have questioned some of Hutton's more over-the-top anecdotes. One said, 'I'm surprised Jimmy could have stayed sober long enough to have remembered some of those things he allegedly did with Freddie.' Similarly, Mike Moran added, 'Jimmy used to get drunk and embarrass everybody and that's why he was never present at a lot of the things he claimed to be.' Other friends have stated that Hutton's book might have been better received had it been co-written with one of Freddie's trusted journalist-allies, such as David Wigg. This almost certainly would have eliminated the over-use of words such as 'gay' and 'husband', wholly acceptable when in their proper context, but overbearing when used as a sensationalist ploy in an attempt to sell books.

In fact, Wigg had been Hutton's first choice, as the journalist himself explained, 'I was going to do a book with Mary and she went cold on me at the last minute. And Jimmy *would* have done his book with me, if I hadn't promised to do Mary's. So in the end I lost out on *both*.'

Even so, though Hutton had not actually put pen to paper, the dialogue and anecdotes – real or invented – were all his, recounted by a man who was entirely comfortable with his sexuality and not afraid of pulling out all the stops.

Mercury and Me contained a fair amount of bad language. 'With Freddie, every other word began with F, but he always made cursing sound so hilarious!' Jackie Gunn recalled. There was a great deal written about what had transpired behind the bedroom door and much of the camp, ribald humour which was an essential ingredient of Freddie's personality but which may not have been appreciated by the parents of younger, more impressionable fans. Freddie's father is also alleged to have become physically ill after being read one particular Hutton anecdote, to which David Evans responded, 'They are going to find anything that's written about their son's "other business", as they called it, offensive because it is going to highlight the fact that he was homosexual, and that's what they cannot bear.'

Controversial Jim Hutton's book may have been. It was also honest in its approach, bursting with compassion and respect for Freddie Mercury the man, and just about every one of the singer's surviving gay friends have maintained that he would have loved it.

Hutton's importance, on the other hand, has been challenged by some, including Queen's chronicler and official biographer, Jim Jenkins, who from his position on the group's periphery was able to draw a more plausible conclusion than most:

> Let's face it, Freddie and Jim *did* have a serious relationship, there's no question of that. But if Freddie loved Jim the way Jim says he did in his book, why didn't he leave him the house? If Jim really was his husband, then Freddie would have regarded him as his next of kin. If you're living in a house with somebody who's been your lover for six years, you don't leave it to a girlfriend from years ago, you leave it to the one you're with now. If Freddie was so much in love with him on his death-bed, why did he only leave him 500 grand? He also left Phoebe and Joe 500 grand, and they only worked for him. If *I* was his lover, I wouldn't be happy getting the same amount as somebody who was an employee.

Again, the truth may never be known.

Another fragmented biography of Freddie which was savaged by the critics and virulently opposed by his friends was Rick Sky's *The Show Must Go On*, though, to be fair, the then pop music editor of the *Daily Mirror* did announce that a proportion of his royalties would be going to the Terrence Higgins Trust. Sky's claim that he had been a friend of the singer was hotly challenged by his real friends. Jackie Gunn declared that the pair had met just once 'When Sky had plonked himself at Freddie's table with a tape-recorder and somebody had conveniently taken a photograph. Freddie absolutely detested the man.' It was also revealed that Sky had written his book five months before Freddie's death, to which Paul Burston of *City Limits* responded, 'And if that doesn't make your blood boil, the not-so-subtle attempts to reclaim Mercury's story as the cautionary tale of a hot-blooded heterosexual who was baited into the homosexual under-world will.'

Sky was one of those journalists condemned by Brian May – 'the mass of opportunist writings . . . carelessly cobbled together by wishful-thinkers claiming (falsely, of course) to have known Freddie intimately' – in his brief introduction to *Queen: As It Began*, the definitive biography of the group which appeared in 1992. The authors, Jackie Gunn and Jim Jenkins, had laboured painstakingly over the script for four years, most of the time wholly unaware that by the time of its completion, the house lights would be fading. Jim Jenkins said, 'The script was ready for being edited in June 1991, then in the August we were told that it would have to be shelved until a later date. We weren't given an explanation, and I only found out two weeks before he died how really ill Freddie was.'

As the text had been completed at the time of Freddie's death, the authors decided not to jump on to the sensationa-lism bandwagon by speculating exactly when Freddie had contracted AIDS. 'To have added such presumptions *after* his death would not have been fair,' Jackie said. 'Freddie had already read the script, and changing so much as a single sentence would have been us letting him down. He deserved better than that.'

On 26 May 1992 Queen's 1986 Wembley concert was released as a double album, completely unedited, and it entered the charts at Number 2. On 16 November, to commemorate the first anniversary of Freddie's death, EMI released 'The Freddie Mercury Album', a compilation of eleven of his solo songs – mostly reworked and remixed tracks from the by now deleted 'Mr Bad Guy' album, except for *Time, In My Defence* and *The Great Pretender*.

Many fans disliked the album because, at just forty-four minutes, they considered it far too short, and also because too many of the songs had been remixed and doctored. Roger Taylor even went as far as denouncing it in Queen's fan club magazine, telling fans, 'I wish to point out that due to certain factors (solo projects) none of the three remaining members of Queen have been involved in any way with the record.' Even so, it was a fine tribute to a great artist, a little long in coming perhaps on account of the essential marketing process, and it reached Number 14 in the hit-parade, earning Freddie a posthumous gold disc. Four months prior to that, *Barcelona* had been re-released as the theme for the Olympic Games Freddie had intended to perform at with Montserrat Caballé. It had reached Number 2.

In the Queen saga, just one chapter remained. After four years of deliberation and wrangling, Freddie's last seven songs were taken from the archives, and the surviving members of the group added their music and backing vocals to the tapes. Several earlier tracks supplied enough material to make up an album, and 'Made In Heaven' was released at the end of 1995 – shooting straight to the top of the charts. It had been a heartbreaking task which had affected all three of them badly. Brian May admitted afterwards, 'This last album is one of the most ridiculously painful experiences I've ever had. I've done it for this album because I thought it was very important to get those last pieces of Freddie out. If it hadn't been for that, I wouldn't have wanted to do it. I valued my life more than the process.'

The sleeve for 'Made In Heaven' and its two subsequent singles, *Heaven For Everyone* and *A Winter's Tale*, was designed by Richard Gray, and though perhaps unethical in the way it was assembled using several of Gray's photographs, it is nevertheless very moving. Brian May, John Deacon and Roger Taylor (photographed in England) stand silhouetted with their backs to the camera in the grounds of the Duck House, gazing across Lake Geneva while to their right stands the statue of Freddie (snapped in a field near Gray's home) which had attracted a great deal of media attention in the months after his death, but which had yet to be assigned a suitable site. It was close to this tranquil spot that Freddie's ashes had been scattered.

With Freddie gone, Queen no longer exist as an active working ensemble, and unless further archive material with Freddie is found and released, they will live on only in our memories and our hearts, and in catalogues. Of Freddie's unreleased work with Montserrat Caballé, there are six songs which can only be made commercially available with her consent, not Queen's. One is a rehearsal of them singing *Music of the Night* from Andrew Lloyd Webber's *Phantom of the Opera*. Montserrat told me, 'Most of these pieces were taped at Freddie's home, and some never got as far as being given titles. There were two pieces that we really liked, and these were recorded in the studio, but we never got around to editing them, so I will never give permission for them to be released.' Michael Jackson similarly owns the copyright to the two tapes he completed with Freddie – *Victory* and *State of Shock* – but has stated that they will not be released. The tape-recording of *We Are the Champions* and the first couplets of *Bohemian Rhapsody* sung in Japanese and dating from 1985, may suffer a similar fate.

Freddie built his life on shifting sands, but his sublime

showmanship and tragically early death have ensured him a place in legend, comparable only to the likes of Presley and Piaf, Dietrich and Dean, and a mere handful of others. 'Queen without Freddie Mercury?' the journalist Tony Parsons once mused. 'Like *Casablanca* without Bogart? Morecambe without Wise? Toad without the hole?'

'Queen will never be an icon, but Freddie *always* will,' David Evans maintains, and he is of course absolutely right. Freddie is completely irreplaceable.

Perhaps the last word should be left to Brian May, who said shortly after his friend's death, 'My personal feeling is that we should never go out and try and be Queen again. It doesn't make sense without Freddie.'

Freddie Mercury Discography

The following represents Freddie Mercury's work on vinyl, video and compact disc. It does not include commercial cassette recordings, picture discs, promos, tapes, CD videos and singles, and bootlegs of out-takes and live recordings which are too numerous to mention.

1973
I Can Hear Music; *Goin' Back* (EMI 2030) Recorded as Larry Lurex

1984
Love Kills; *Rotwang's Party** (CBS A4735) *Not sung by Freddie Mercury

1985
I Was Born to Love You; *Stop All The Fighting* (CBS A6019)

MR BAD GUY: *Let's Turn It On*; *Made in Heaven*; *I Was Born to Love You*; *Foolin' Around*; *Your Kind of Lover*; *Mr Bad Guy*; *Man-Made Paradise*; *There Must Be More to Life*

Than This; *Living On My Own*; *My Love is Dangerous*; *Love Me Like There's No Tomorrow* (CBS 86312)

Made in Heaven; *She Blows Hot and Cold* (CBS A6413)

Living On My Own; *My Love is Dangerous* (CBS A6555)

Love Me Like There's No Tomorrow; *Let's Turn It On* (CBS A6725)

1986
Time; *Time* (instrumental) (EMI 5559)

1987
The Great Pretender; *Exercises in Free Love* (PARLO-PHONE R6151)

*Barcelona**; *Exercise in Free Love*** (POLYDOR PO887)
1988
*The Golden Boy**; *The Fallen Priest** (POLYDOR PO23)

BARCELONA: *Barcelona**; *La Japonaise**; *The Fallen Priest**; *Ensueno**; *The Golden Boy**; *Guide Me Home**; *How Can I Go On?***; *Overture Piccante** (POLYDOR POLH44)

1989
*How Can I Go On?***; *Overture Piccante** (POLYDOR PO29)

1992
*Barcelona**; *Exercises in Free Love*** (POLYDOR PO 221)

* Sung with Montserrat Caballé
** Sung by Montserrat Caballé

How Can I Go On?*; *The Golden Boy** (POLYDOR PO234)
In My Defence: *Love Kills* (EMI R6331)

THE FREDDIE MERCURY ALBUM: *The Great Pretender*; *Foolin' Around*; *Time*; *Your Kind Of Lover*; *Exercises in Free Love*; *In My Defence*; *Mr Bad Guy*; *Let's Turn It On*; *Living On My Own*; *Love Kills*; *Barcelona** (PARLO-PHONE 7809992)

1993
The Great Pretender; *Stop All the Fighting* (EMI R6336)

Living On My Own; *Living On My Own* (Mixes) (EMI 6355)

VIDEOS
FREDDIE MERCURY: THE VIDEO EP: *I Was Born To Love You*; *Made In Heaven*; *Living On My Own*; *Time* (1986, PMI MXS 9900552)

THE GREAT PRETENDER: *The Great Pretender* (7'' version); *The Great Pretender* (extended version) (1987 PMI MVW 9900662)

BARCELONA: *Barcelona**; *The Golden Boy**; *How Can I Go On?**

---

* Sung with Montserrat Caballé
** Sung by Montserrat Caballé

Index